Introduction to

PUBLIC

ADMINISTRATION

Carl J. Gabrini, Ph.D. and Grace Adams-Square, Ph.D.

ISBN: 978-1-959203-16-2

Produced by:
University System of Georgia

Published by:
University of North Georgia Press
Dahlonega, Georgia

Cover Design and Layout Design:
Corey Parson

For more information, please visit http://ung.edu/university-press
Or email ungpress@ung.edu
Instructor Resources available upon request.

Table of Contents

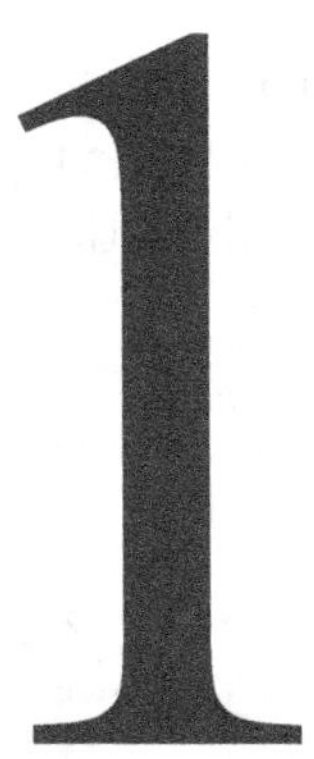

Introduction to Public Administration

LEARNING OBJECTIVES

Students studying this chapter should be able to:

1. Define the field of public administration.
2. Distinguish between public administration and business administration.
3. Explain why studying public administration is important.
4. Describe the division of topics by chapter in the textbook.

INTRODUCTION

When initially studying a subject, it is helpful to identify and learn its important terminology before diving deeper. This approach helps understanding in three ways: it frames the subject, identifies some of its primary divisions, and aids comprehension. With that in mind, before we begin exploring some its topics, we will first define "public administration" to build our foundation for its study and establish a useful context. We will start by dividing public administration into two separate definitions and explore their individual meanings before considering what they mean when combined. Following this, we will contrast public administration and business administration, which will help us when we examine the importance of studying public administration. Finally, we will summarize the topics covered in subsequent chapters. Since this is an introductory text, we will not cover all the topics associated with public administration. Instead, we will focus on those topics we consider foundational, and that will provide you with a solid basis for further study.

It is essential to remind the readers that this text focuses on public administration within the United States. While the study of public administration has international, comparative, and historical dimensions, these are beyond the scope of this introductory textbook. However, we will address some aspects of the intellectual history of public administration in the U.S. to help frame the topics we discuss. For more in-depth exploration, students are encouraged to pursue those courses entirely devoted to studying this subject in depth. Our aim here is to provide enough context to give students an appreciation of public administration here in the U.S.

WHAT IS PUBLIC ADMINISTRATION?

Our topic consists of two words rather than one: "public" and "administration." The word "public" can function as both a noun and adjective. As an adjective, it has two primary meanings, both of which apply to our use of the word: (1) "exposed to general view, open, well known, prominent," and (2) "of or relating to a government or being in the service of the community or nation." Further, it refers to "people in general, universal, or relating to business or community interests as opposed to private affairs" (Merriam-Webster, 2003).

Administration is defined as "performance of executive duties, management, the act or process of administering, the execution of public affairs as distinguished from policymaking" (Merriam-Webster, 2003). Based on our review of these definitions, we can summarize our understanding of public administration as an activity focused on running government and acting in such a way as likely to affect all or some subgroup of citizens. This activity, moreover, is likely to be transparent and open to the public it affects.

Academics studying and writing about public administration have contributed various definitions of public administration. One of the challenges in defining public administration is its relationship to public policy. Public policy generally consists of acts originating from the legislative bodies or statements by the chief executive of government, such as executive orders. Additionally, some point to the courts as being a source of public policy through their case decisions. Others focus on the process agencies use to establish those regulations necessary to implementing the laws and orders of elected leaders. Some posit that, rather than merely implementing the laws and orders affecting their programs and function, agency processes for adopting regulations can create new public policy. Because new policy created in this way is outside of electoral politics, it might never be subject to the same scrutiny as the acts of elected leaders. However, adopting regulations is a necessary part of the administrative process.

Woodrow Wilson (1887) describes administration as "government in action" and defines public administration as the "detailed and systematic execution of public law." Nearly forty years later, White (1926) defines public administration as using people and resources to accomplish the goals of government (p. 2). He includes the idea that government is accountable for economy and efficiency when using public resources. These early definitions shift the focus of studying politics and policymaking toward the managerial functions involved in running government operations. Dimock et al. (1936) further describes public administration as "effectuating community business" (p. 1). Later definitions recognize the importance of capturing all sides of public administration and recognizing its managerial and political nature.

Shafritz's *Dictionary of Public Policy and Administration* (2004) includes definitions for both "public" and "administration" as well as their combined usage. He defines public administration broadly as "whatever government does" and as the "law in action." Other portions of the definition include: "regulation," "the executive function," the act of "organizing and managing people and other resources to achieve the goals of government," "implementing the public interest," "the art and science of applying management to the public sector," and, lastly, "use of managerial, political, and legal theories and processes to fulfill legislative, executive, and judicial governmental mandates for the provision of regulatory and service functions of society as a whole or for some segments of it."

Modern public administration has multiple dimensions, making it a challenge to define in a single sentence or statement. Shafritz et al. (2016) approach this complexity by defining public administration through eighteen different statements and across four dimensions: political, legal, managerial, and occupational. The following table illustrates how they organize the statements around the four dimensions.

Table 1: Shafritz et al. Dimensions and Statements Defining Public Administration

Political	Legal	Managerial	Occupational
Public administration is what government does.	Public administration is the law in action.	Public administration is the executive function in government.	Public administration is an occupational category.
Public administration is both direct and indirect.	Public administration is regulation.	Public administration is a management specialty.	Public administration is an essay contest. (Refers to the power of the written word.)
Public administration is a phase in the public policymaking cycle.	Public administration is "The King's Largesse." (Refers to bestowing goods, services, or honors on others.)	Public administration is "Mickey Mouse." (Refers to red tape)	Public administration is idealism in action.
Public administration is implementing the public interest.	Public administration is theft.	Public administration is art, not science— or vice versa.	Public administration is an academic field.
Public administration is doing collectively that which cannot be done well individually.			Public administration is a profession.

The dimensions and statements capture the multifaceted nature of public administration, including the public's positive and negative attitudes, its political and technical dimensions, its inherently bureaucratic nature, and the high degree of professionalism required of those who serve in the various agencies, departments, and offices.

HOW IS PUBLIC ADMINISTRATION DIFFERENT FROM BUSINESS ADMINISTRATION?

It is not unusual to hear statements equating public organizations with private businesses. But are these statements fair? Are there fundamental differences between public entities and private businesses? In this section, we will examine these differences, because acknowledging these types of organizations as different is important to knowing how the administrative function in each should be approached.

A novel way for students to approach answering this question is by using ChatGPT, a relatively new artificial intelligence (AI) tool that has received mixed reviews in academia. The authors believe that, when used appropriately, AI can serve as a valuable resource in academic coursework. As an example, students can use an official account set up through OpenAI, the company that created ChatGPT, to type "government vs. private business" into the search bar and press enter. The AI then generates a succinct summary of differences between these two sectors, public and private, including ownership, goals, accountability, funding, decision-making, regulations, and culture (OpenAI, 2023a).

Ownership

How does the concept of ownership differ between private and public sector organizations? Private businesses are owned by individuals. Sole proprietorships are truly owned by a single individual, while partnership—considered as pass-through organizations for tax purposes—are owned by two or more individuals. Corporations, formed through state regulation, are authorized to issue stock to individuals referred to as shareholders. These corporations can be closely held or publicly traded on exchanges such as the New York Stock Exchange or NASDAQ.

In contrast, government in the United States does not have ownership in the traditional sense. Its authority and legitimacy originate from a constitution (Goodnow, 2003). The U.S. has a federal Constitution, while each of the fifty states operates under its own constitution. Local government authority originates out of the state constitutions and is further defined through charters at the county and municipal levels. The United States, as a democratic republic, is guided by founding principles stated most clearly in the Declaration of Independence and the Federalist Papers. These principles guided the formation of the many constitutions that serve as the backbone of public administration.

Goals

The goal of all private businesses is to increase shareholder value by, among other things, earning accounting profits over time. A private business's interest in such other activities as Environment, Social, and Governance (ESG); Diversity, Equity, and Inclusion (DEI); and Corporate Social Responsibility (CSR) is also driven by the profit motive but focusing more on a long-term versus short-term perspective. Businesses offer products and services to consumers with the goal of maximizing the profit they earn or minimizing their losses.

Government, on the other hand, exists to provide law and order, justice, security (both internal and external), prosperity, property rights, and the public good. It is difficult to fully encapsulate the goal of government in a single sentence, so others may take issue with this description. However we believe it captures the essential role that government fulfills in the United States through its various policies and programs.

Accountability

Private businesses are accountable to those we define as owners or shareholders. The distance between decisions and ownership grows as one moves from sole proprietorships to the corporate form of organization. In corporations, shareholders are represented by a corporate board that oversees the business's operations. The board's role is to ensure that management is in the interests of the shareholders. Businesses use systems of internal controls and enterprise risk management to ensure accountability in achieving the organization's mission.

Government is accountable to citizens. Those responsible for administration are accountable to the elected or appointed leaders of the three branches of government (executive, legislative, and judicial). Government organizations are often described as bureaucratic because of the nature of public accountability. Ultimately, citizens hold government accountable through public elections. The elected leaders are responsible for appointing those in charge of the various agencies, departments, and offices that constitute governments at all levels.

Funding

Private businesses are funded in primarily three ways: (1) owners contributing capital (cash and/or property), (2) borrowed funds, either through loans or bonds, and (3) revenue earned through the sale of their products and services. Additionally, cash can be generated in other ways as a business matures and experiences periods of expansion or contraction, often through the sale of assets. Capital contributed by owners is especially important during the initial startup phase of a business. Ultimately, sales revenue is considered the highest quality of funding available to a business and is often used as a measure when evaluating a business's success. Borrowed funds are used strategically at various points throughout the life of a business.

The public sector relies primarily on taxes levied on citizens to cover the cost of government. Additionally, governments charge fees for various services, such as vehicle registrations, driver's licenses, hunting and fishing permits, and public park admissions. The primary difference between how a governments and private businesses raise funds is in choice. Consumers can choose whether to buy or not buy, and lenders can choose whether to lend or not lend. Citizens, however, do not have the freedom to choose whether to pay their tax obligations. We often refer to this lack of choice as coercion.

Decision-Making

Private businesses generally make decisions that are in the best interests of owners or shareholders. Boards and senior management generally focus on strategic or long-range decisions. Senior management also works closely with other levels of management to make operational decisions that are short-term but support the long-range strategic plan. In general, decision-makers in private businesses have a greater degree of discretion than those in the public sector.

Government decision-making is inherently more complex. At the highest levels of government, decisions are made by elected officials through complex legislative and executive processes. While these processes may not always appear efficient, they are designed to protect the country and citizens from the abuse of power. Administrative decisions, in turn, are made through a complex regulatory process. At the lowest levels of government, decisions are generally governed by law and regulation, leaving little room for discretion on the part of the decision-maker.

Regulations

Private businesses operate under a regulatory framework consisting of federal, state, and local laws, regulations, and rules. Private business operators often refer to this framework as "red tape," because they see it as tying their hands and making it more difficult to run their businesses. These regulations impact every aspect of a business, including how it manages relationships with employees to how it manufactures its products as well as conducts its services.

Government creates a regulatory framework but is generally not accountable for operating under the regulations it creates. It can grant itself exceptions, even under circumstances where the regulations may apparently apply to all sectors of the economy.

Culture

The private sector is generally more competitive in nature than the public sector. Private businesses compete with one another when they operate in similar industries, such as fast food. This competitive environment often encourages businesses to behave opaquely, sharing only the information required by law. In contrast, government is typically required to operate transparently. Government actions and decisions are often made in open forums unless specifically exempted by public law.

Private business culture is defined by the profit motive mentioned earlier. Businesses are more open to innovation but focus on economy, effectiveness, and efficiency. Economy refers to how the organizational resources are used or employed in running the business. Efficiency describes the relationship between inputs and outputs, with businesses seeking to use only the necessary inputs to generate the desired outputs. Effectiveness has to do with outcomes, or the achievement of the businesses mission.

The government does not ignore economy, efficiency, and effectiveness in managing its affairs, but its mission often requires decisions and actions that do not effect an increase in any of these three objectives. The bureaucratic structure of government often makes it difficult to increase economy and efficiency in delivering their programs and services. Instead, the government often must focus on such goals as equality, equity, stability, and consistency. These objectives do not always, or often, align with economical and efficient use of resources.

We can also examine the differences between public organizations and private business enterprises by comparing their mission statements, as found in social media and stakeholder messaging, and their annual reports. We define stakeholders here as including primarily citizens within each government's jurisdiction and the owners or shareholders of private businesses. To illustrate this point, consider a comparison between a large publicly traded corporation, such as McDonald's, and a state government, like Georgia. We will examine them through their strategic planning and financial reporting documents. For McDonald's Corporation, we accessed its mission statement and shareholder communications through its website and the investor link to investors at the top right of its homepage. McDonald's states on its website: "Our mission is to make delicious feel-good moments easy for everyone" (2022).

McDonald's further states, "Our strategy is underpinned by our focus on running great restaurants, empowering our people and getting faster, more innovative and more efficient at solving problems for our customers and people." Digging a little deeper into their annual report, we read about McDonald's business model: "the company is primarily a franchisor and believes franchising is paramount to delivering great-tasting food, locally relevant customer experiences and driving profitability." As a private business enterprise, McDonald's mission is fundamentally tied to profitability.

In contrast, the State of Georgia (n.d.) includes no mention of profitability in its strategic planning or financial reporting documents. On the Governor's Office website, there is no single mission statement for the state. Instead, the focus is on a vision statement and a set of goals. The vision for the State of Georgia is: "Put hardworking Georgians first through streamlined, accessible, and fiscally responsible government."

Several strategic goals are tied to this vision:

1. Make Georgia number one for small business.

2. Reform state government.

3. Strengthen rural Georgia.

4. Put Georgians first.

These goals are further broken down into specific objectives within the Governor's strategic plan. Additional search of the government's website reveals multiple mission statements for individual units of state government. While government is often perceived as a centralized bureaucracy, a certain amount of decentralization results from the division of powers within our democratic republic. It is important to keep in mind that the focus in the public sector shifts from profitability to effectiveness, efficiency, economy, and compliance. This contextual difference affects how leaders lead, managers manage, and administrators administer. It also affects how we will approach our discussion of public administration.

A question for students to consider: Is there a difference between leadership, management, and administration? (Class Discussion Suggestion).

WHY IS IT IMPORTANT TO STUDY PUBLIC ADMINISTRATION?

The United States comprises many governments operating within a vast web of jurisdictions, each with unique and sometimes overlapping responsibilities. While most people know there is one federal and fifty state governments, there are also over 90,000 local governments across the United States. These include over 3,000 counties, more than 19,000 municipalities, over 16,000 townships, and more than 51,000 special-purpose governments (Federalism US, 2020). Federal and state governments share powers as outlined by the U.S. Constitution. The remaining governments derive their authority from the states and their constitutions, which determine exactly what they can do.

Counties are generally subdivisions, relied on by states to deliver certain services that are better managed locally rather than centrally by the state. In states with larger counties, these may be further subdivided into townships. Municipalities are incorporated by their citizens under state law and usually offer a more comprehensive slate of services than those provided by counties. Special-purpose governments, in contrast, generally focus on a limited set of services, such as fire protection, education, water, or electricity, unlike general-purpose governments like municipalities.

Citizens rely on the government to provide a broad range of services (Burns, 1994). There are significant overlapping responsibilities among different levels of government. Some programs may result from laws passed at the federal level and flowed down through the states to the local governments, while others may be passed at the state level and flowed down to the local governments. We depend on the government for essential aspects of life, including healthcare, education, public safety, national security, economic development, and general wellbeing. In addition to providing services, the government regulates private organizations that provide goods and services to citizens. These regulations cover areas such as the food and drugs we consume, the energy powering our communities, and many other services offered to the public.

Property owners in states like Florida and Louisiana rely on state governments to provide property insurance because private insurance companies often are unwilling to write certain policies in areas most prone to hurricane-related losses (Citizens Insurance, 2021). The government also provides unemployment insurance for those who lose their jobs and healthcare for those individuals' employer-based coverage. Additionally, the government regulates critical areas such as immigration and citizenship, national security—including cybersecurity— utilities (electricity, water, and telecommunications), housing, education, land use and development, and transportation. One of many pressing issues facing the government is the repair and replacement of the nation's aging infrastructure, including bridges, tunnels, seaports, airports, and interstates. Funds are being set aside to deal with the deterioration and outdated condition of these critical components of the nation's infrastructure.

Examples of current policy topics of particular concern to citizens and all levels of government include law enforcement and immigration. These issues cut across political, social, and economic dimensions of society. Across the country, tensions between citizens and law enforcement continue to simmer. Issues such as profiling and use of force have raised concerns about police officer behavior and the targeting of specific groups within the population. Focus on the behavior of law enforcement is nothing new in our society. From the earliest parts of U.S. history to the present, people have remained critical of law enforcement's commitment to protecting and serving all individuals, regardless of differences (OpenAI, 2023b).

- Slavery Era and Reconstruction Period (1619–1877): Laws that required the use of local police to track down and return runaway slaves to owners.

- Jim Crow Era (1877–1968): Use of local and state law enforcement to enforce laws designed to maintain the institution of segregation.

- Civil Rights Movement and Post-Civil Rights Era (1950s–1980s): Local and state law enforcement were involved in putting down civil rights marches and protests.

- Contemporary Issues: Beginning in 1990s and continuing to the current year, we continue to hear about tense interactions between police and members of the Black community, with some incidents involving violence and the death of citizens.

More contemporary issues started with the beating of Rodney King in 1992, the death of Trayvon Martin in 2012, and more recent events such as the death of George Floyd and Ahmaud Arbery in 2020. The long list of violent interactions has led to people questioning the ethics and behavior of police officers. The history of tensions between citizens and law enforcement has given rise to calls to defund and radically change the law enforcement function in the United States. This problem has yet to be resolved, often becoming dormant until reignited by the events that spark public outrage and calls for justice.

Concern over immigration policy is as old as the nation itself. As a nation of immigrants, the United States has experienced several waves of immigration throughout its history. Today's version of the debate centers on illegal immigration and the overall number of immigrants allowed into the country through various immigration programs.

What are the major issues associated with our current debate over immigration policy? This is another good question that you can initially ask ChatGPT. Why not sign into ChatGPT, type in the question, and see what you get back? The results of this search are presented below as we close out this section of the first chapter (OpenAI, 2023c).

- Border Security: This includes debates over the adequate funding of U.S. Customs and Border Protection. Topics of this debate include the construction of the southern border wall, the use of technology, and the number of border patrol officers.

- Legal Immigration: This involves the current laws and policies allowing people to immigrate legally to the United States. Immigration policy sets limits on the number of people allowed into the country.

- Refugee and Asylum Policies: This addresses how the United States treats individuals seeking admission to flee violence and persecution in their home countries.

- Pathways to Citizenship: One of the major discussions in this area involves the "Dreamers" program, but it involves all programs that allow people legal entry to the United States. Some programs allow temporary residence, while others provide a pathway to citizenship.

- Enforcement Measures: One of the big debates around this issue involves states that allow cities to declare themselves as "sanctuary cities," which refuse to enforce immigration laws that result in the detention and deportation of undocumented immigrants.

During the first Trump administration, the government engaged Part 42 of the 1944 The Public Health Services Act (Ellis & Kuhn, 2023). This act empowered the CDC to close immigration of certain groups during national health emergencies. It was used to stop the flow of immigration into the United States during and after the pandemic. As of May 2023, the act expired, and immigration has since restarted in earnest.

HOW IS THE REST OF THE BOOK ORGANIZED?

This textbook introduces public administration to those interested in pursuing leadership careers in the public sector. But what is public administration? According to *Merriam-Webster*, it is "a branch of political science dealing primarily with the structure and workings of agencies charged with the administration of governmental functions." These agencies include federal, state, and local governments as well as some not-for-profit organizations. They report to elected government leaders through constitutional authority, legal mandates, or contractual, or grant conditions.

While public and private organizations share many of the same features, public administration has some unique features. Take the movie *The Truman Show* for an example. It tells the story of Truman, a man whose entire life is being broadcast as a reality TV show—without his knowledge—watched the world over. By the movie's end, Truman figures out his life is a public spectacle and engineers a climactic escape from his encapsulated world. Once you work in the public sector for a while, you might imagine yourself feeling like Truman.

Transparency is probably the most unique feature of a public administration career, one without equal in the private sector. Often referred to as "operating in the sunshine," this emphasis on openness and public scrutiny has its roots in the purging of government employees accused of being communists in the 1950s. This and other actions of the federal government ultimately led to the passage of the *Freedom of Information Act* (FOIA) in 1966. This led to all fifty states enacting their own laws governing public access to government records. These laws, as amended over time, have helped define the work environment for public managers.

For students entering upon graduation and preparing to assume leadership positions in public organizations, understanding this environment is crucial. It will shape and influence every decision you make, every action you take, and everything you say or write.

Regardless of one's profession, competence is important. However, in public administration, the added pressure of leading in the open—fully exposed to criticism and second-guessing—heightens its importance. This text intends to provide students with the foundational knowledge needed to develop competence in public administration. The book begins with this introduction and is followed by nine chapters introducing topics the authors deem important to developing competence and being an effective 21st-century government leader.

Chapter two provides an overview of the foundations of public administration in the United States. It includes a discussion of the constitutional foundations of public administration and the role of public administrators in operationalizing the missions assigned to various government units. The chapter also discusses different approaches to public administration and addresses career path options.

Chapter three focuses on bureaucracy—often described as "red tape." This chapter examines the tension between democracy and bureaucracy as well as the various approaches to organizing a bureaucracy.

Chapter four shifts focus to the topic of ethics in public administration. Leaders in our democratic society are entrusted with a sacred duty to uphold and defend the Constitution upon which the nation is founded. Citizens expect both elected and appointed leaders to conduct governmental affairs in an ethical manner.

This discussion continues in chapter five, which addresses the importance of efficiency and effectiveness in government. Public administrators are held accountable for program outcomes and the responsible stewardship of resources used to achieve those outcomes. Additionally, administrators are also responsible for safeguarding organizational assets. To do so, they must be familiar with waste, fraud, and abuse, as well as the internal controls designed to prevent or detect such misbehavior.

Chapter six introduces students to the intellectual history of public administration. Rather than being static, this history is dynamic, one that has evolved over time, often following the shifts in society, the economy, national values, and strategic and operational challenges. This chapter illustrates the close linkage between theory and practice in public administration.

Closely related to the evolution of public administration paradigms are the challenges leaders face when making decisions, which is the subject of chapter seven. This chapter addresses not only the challenges in making decisions but also of making sure those decisions are acted upon and how best to evaluate the outcomes.

Chapter eight introduces students to managing human resources in the public sector. One of an administrator's chief assets is their staff. Recruiting, developing, and retaining talent are important for effective operation of organizations. Even well-made decisions require competent and well-trained staff to ensure their proper implementation. Managing people in the public sector has become even more important due to the increasing number of retirements and intense competition for a smaller pool of new job market entrants.

Chapter nine covers the important topic of public policy. Earlier in Chapter Six, we addressed the challenges in decision-making. In government, decisions are often formulated into policy positions that become part of legislation considered by Congress, regulations adopted by agencies, or orders issued by the Executive Branch. This chapter introduces students to how policies are developed and implemented, along with the tools used to evaluate them.

Chapter ten serves as a conclusion or summary, in which the authors discuss the interconnectedness of the topics covered, offer thoughts on the future of public administration, and summarize the challenges and opportunities government leaders face in the 21st Century.

As this textbook reaches completion in 2023, we can reflect on the importance of public administration during the COVID-19 pandemic, which has gripped the world since late 2019. By mid-2021, there were signs beginning to indicate that the worst was over. However, the pandemic reinforced the importance of competence and the challenges public administrators face by operating "in the sunshine." The pandemic has placed immense strain on the national, state, and local economies, healthcare systems, and individual households. Government leaders have had to work closely across the various levels of government, among agencies within the same level, and with the private sector to address the unprecedented challenges brought on by the crisis.

As an example, one of the most significant challenges government leaders faced during the COVID-19 pandemic was encouraging and coordinating the development and distribution of vaccines. These challenges were not only faced by leaders in the United States but also by leaders all over the world. The effectiveness of leadership decisions and their performance in combating the pandemic will be argued, debated, and reflected upon for decades to come.

Regardless, faced with a public health crisis, our public leaders and their staff needed to act. They needed to perform in face the unrelenting public scrutiny, criticism, and second-guessing from rivals, the media, citizens, and other governments. A career in public service—leading a unit of government—can be both challenging and immensely worthwhile. It is a noble profession whose rewards are not always measured in monetary terms. Often, the reward is knowing that you did the best you could with what you had under the given circumstances, and with good motives.

REFERENCES

Burns, N. (1994). *The formation of American local governments: Private values in public institutions*. Oxford University Press. New York, NY.

Citizens Insurance. (2021, December 19). In *Wikipedia*. https://en.wikipedia.org/wiki/Citizens_Insurance

Ellis, N. & Kuhn, C. (2023, January 13). What is Title 42 and what does it mean for immigration at the southern border? *PBS News*. https://www.pbs.org/newshour/nation/what-is-title-42-and-what-does-it-mean-for-immigration-at-the-southern-border

Federalism US. (2020). *Significant features of American federalism: 1.1 number of government jurisdictions*. https://federalism.us/significantfeatures2020/1-1-number-of-government-jurisdictions/

Gaus, J. M., White, L. D., & Dimock, M. E. (1936). *The frontiers of public administration*. Russell & Russell. New York, NY.

Goodnow, F. J. (2003). *A study in government: Politics and administration*. Transaction Publishers. New Brunswick, NJ.

Merriam-Webster. (2003). Administration. In *Merriam-Webster's collegiate dictionary* (11th ed., 16). Merriam-Webster, Incorporated.

Merriam-Webster. (2003). Public. In *Merriam-Webster's collegiate dictionary* (11th ed., 1005). Merriam-Webster, Incorporated.

McDonald's Corporation. (2022). *2022 annual report*. https://corporate.mcdonalds.com/content/dam/sites/corp/nfl/pdf/MCD_2023_Annual_Report.pdf

OpenAI. (2023). *ChatGPT* (May 24 version) [Large Language Model]. https://chat.openai.com/chat/

Shafritz, J. M. (2004). *The dictionary of public policy and administration* (236–238).

Shafritz, J. M., Russell, E. W., Borick, C. P., and Hyde, A. C. (2016). *Introducing public administration*. Routledge. New York, NY.

State of Georgia (n.d.). *State organizations*. Retrieved March 13, 2023, from https://georgia.gov/state-organizations

Washington Post. (2023, May 1). Rate of fatal police shootings in the United States from 2015 to May 2023, by ethnicity (per million of the population per year) [Graph]. In *Statista*. Retrieved May 22, 2023, from https://www.statista.com/statistics/1123070/police-shootings-rate-ethnicity-us/

The Library of Congress. (n.d.). *Official U.S. executive branch web sites*. Retrieved March 13, 2023, from https://www.loc.gov/rr/news/fedgov.html

White, L. D. (1926). *Introduction to the study of public administration*. The MacMillan Company. New York, NY.

Wilson, W. T. (1887). The study of administration. *Political Science Quarterly*, 2(2), 197–222.

The White House. (n.d.). Local government. *State and local government*. Retrieved March 13, 2023, from https://www.whitehouse.gov/about-the-white-house/our-government/state-local-government/

The Constitutional and Legislative Foundations of U.S. Public Administration

LEARNING OBJECTIVES

Students studying this chapter should be able to:

1. Discuss the influence of the U.S. Constitution on the field of public administration.

2. Explain the statutory origins of federal agencies and the historical evolution of the president's cabinet and executive independent agencies.

3. Compare the origin, history, and mission of different executive-level agencies.

4. Describe the role of congressional oversight of federal executive-level agencies.

5. Identify and use sources of information to learn about careers in public administration.

INTRODUCTION

If one examines an organizational chart of the U.S. government, one learns that there is more to government than Congress, the president, and the Supreme Court. A complex maze of departments and agencies carry out most of the government's day-to-day operations. This administrative apparatus is likely the part of government most citizens and noncitizens will interact with during their lifetimes. As students of public administration in the U.S., one should understand the origins, history, and role played by these departments and agencies, particularly for those aspiring to a career in public service.

We cannot deeply explore the complex subject of administration and administrative law in the twenty-plus pages of this chapter. However, we will provide an overview and offer suggested readings for those interested in further, more in-depth study. The administrative arm of the federal government owes its existence to interpretations of the Constitution and the exercise of Congress's lawmaking power. Limitations on the use of that administrative power result from struggles between the branches of government and judicial decisions. Oversight of this administrative power is based on interpretation, tradition, and legislation, and we will briefly touch on these topics in this chapter.

John Adams, writing in 1776, noted that the best form of government is one based on law rather than men. The U.S. was founded on this principle, as evidenced by a reading of the Declaration of Independence and the Constitution. The administrative apparatus of the government, therefore, finds its origin in law. While not specifically addressed in the Constitution, the maze of departments and agencies was on the minds of the Constitution's drafters. Rather than addressing this structure in the foundational document, they left its creation to future leaders to create an administration best suited to the nation's needs.

This chapter will introduce how the administrative structure of the federal government came into existence and provide context for its macro-level functions. It will conclude with a discussion of the role of public administrators in running the departments and agencies that carry out the laws passed by Congress and signed by the president. Specifically, we will first address the constitutional foundations, then examine the statutory foundations, and summarize oversight of the administrative apparatus. Finally, the chapter will conclude with a brief discussion of careers in public administration.

CONSTITUTIONAL FOUNDATIONS OF U.S. PUBLIC ADMINISTRATION

The preamble to the U.S. Constitution clearly lays out the objectives of the nation's leaders in forming the new government in 1789:

> We the people of the United States, in order to form a *more perfect Union,* *establish justice, insure domestic tranquility, provide for the common* *defense, promote the general welfare,* and *secure the blessings of liberty* *to ourselves and our posterity,* do ordain and establish this Constitution for the United States of America (U.S. Const. pmbl).

The Preamble (emphasis added), referring to a "more perfect union," paints a picture of citizens living peacefully within a nation of states melded together under one national government—one that would govern impartially, fairly, and even-handedly. The reference to "domestic tranquility" gives the impression that citizens will live in relative peace under stable leadership and orderly transitions of power.

"Common defense" refers to maintaining a national military, as opposed to individual states maintaining their own forces. The cost and organization of this military would be shared among the states but run by the national government.

"General welfare" refers to protecting citizens' rights to pursue their own interests and enjoy prosperity and success. While it does not guarantee success or prosperity for all, it ensures the protection of a system that would allow one to pursue these things.

Finally, the "blessings of liberty" include independence, self-governance, and the freedoms granted through the U.S. system of government.

The balance of the Constitution, without considering the amendments, describes the structure, roles, and functions of each major branch of government, effectively establishing the separation of powers. It also establishes the initial relationship between the federal government and individual states. However, the Constitution is relatively silent on the administrative concerns of governance.

Some may view this as a problem, while others may see it as an opportunity. It is a problem for those who believe the Constitution is static or fixed, requiring strict adherence to the original language. From this perspective, much of what our government does today is extra-Constitutional—a violation of the intent of the original framers. However, this argument does not account for the fact that interpretation is both necessary and implied through the existence of our judicial system.

Conversely, those who view the Constitution as flexible consider this an opportunity. To them, the Constitution was intended to evolve over time as circumstances dictate. This view sees our government as a living, breathing organism, capable of growing and maturing as situations warrant.

Article II, Section 2 of the U.S. Constitution gives us an early glimpse of the acknowledgement and existence of an administrative bureaucracy. The first paragraph of this section states, "he [referring to the president] may require the opinion, in writing, of the principal officer in each of the executive departments, upon any subject relating to the duties of their respective offices . . . ."

In the second paragraph, we read, "He [again, the president] shall have power, by and with the advice and consent of the Senate . . . [to] appoint . . . all other officers of the United States, whose appointments are not herein otherwise provided for, and which shall be established by law." The clause further includes, " . . . but the Congress may by law vest the appointment of such inferior officers, as they think proper, in the president alone . . . or in the heads of departments."

From this language, we can conclude that the framers of the Constitution envisioned an administrative apparatus under the president's authority, with responsibility over various policy areas. It also suggests that there are at least two tiers of officers—superior and inferior—each requiring different methods of appointment. This two-tier system is mentioned again in the Twenty-Fifth Amendment to the Constitution, referring to the role of superior officers in declaring a president unable to discharge the duties of the office.

Further, a search of Supreme Court decisions indicates an important case history addressing this administrative apparatus reporting to the president, such as *U.S. v. Germaine, 1878*. This chapter intends to impress upon the reader the Constitution's foundational role in shaping public administration in the United States. While not intended to be an exhaustive theoretical argument, the evidence suggests that administrative governance was clearly in the minds of both the Constitution's framers and the authors of subsequent amendments.

The Constitution divides power among three branches of government: legislative, executive, and judicial. Lawmaking primarily falls under Congress, with most legislation originating in the House of Representatives (*The White House b*, n.d.). The Judiciary, headed by the U.S. Supreme Court, is largely responsible for presiding over legal cases—some civil, some criminal—and rendering decisions or overseeing the process while juries decide on the outcomes (*The White House c*, n.d.).

The president's responsibilities are divided into three general areas: (1) head of state, (2) head of government, and (3) commander-in-chief of the armed forces (*The White House a*, n.d.). In serving as head of state, the president manages our relationships with other nations. As the head of government, the president executes and enforces those laws passed by Congress. As commander-in-chief, the president oversees all branches of the armed forces, including the reserves, and, when called into service, the National Guard.

According to *The White House* website, the president oversees fifteen executive departments, whose heads are part of the president's cabinet and are responsible for managing the daily affairs of government. Beyond the executive departments, there are at least 96 independent executive units and 220 components within the executive departments. These numbers, however, often vary depending on the source—according to an article in *Forbes Magazine* (2017).

Each of these executive units can trace their origin to a specific legislative action. While the Constitution may be silent on the exact details of how the executive branch is to be structured, it is not quiet on the framers' intent that there be an administrative structure. Rather than dictating specifics through the Constitution, they appear to have left these details to be determined by those would come after them and serve in the government created through the Constitution's adoption.

Table 2.1: Executive Branch

Central Trunk	Main Branches	Independent Agencies
The President and Vice President	Cabinet Departments	Not in Cabinet
• The president leads the entire branch and sets its direction. • The vice president supports the president and takes over if needed.	• There are 15 cabinet departments each with a secretary leading it. • These departments handle broad areas like defense, education, or treasury. • Each department has its own sub-agencies that focus on specific tasks. • Imagine these as major branches stemming from the central trunk.	• There are numerous independent agencies outside the cabinet structure. • These agencies address specific needs, like the CIA or the Environmental Protection Agency (EPA). • Think of these as additional branches growing from the main trunk, but separate from the cabinet departments.

The U.S. Constitution establishes not only a separation of powers among the branches of government but also a system of checks and balances. In *Federalist Papers No. 51*, James Madison asked the question, "To what expedient, then, shall we finally resort, for maintaining in practice the necessary partition of power among the several departments, as laid down in the Constitution?"

Madison followed the question with what he described as "the only answer," writing:

> . . . that all these exterior provisions are found to be inadequate, the defect must be supplied, but so contriving the interior structure of the government as that its several constituent parts may, by their mutual relations, be the means of keeping each other in their proper places.

Madison argues that the checks and balances are embedded in the system itself. By establishing individual organizational units with their own scopes of authority or jurisdiction, no single branch can impose itself on another. Madison states that the "separate and distinct exercise of the different powers of government . . . is essential to the preservation of liberty."

One such control is the presidential veto, established in Article 1, Section 7, Clause 2 of the Constitution. This clause describes the interaction between Congress and the president in passing laws. Once a bill is passed by both houses of Congress, it is sent to the president for consideration. The president can either sign the bill into law or return it to Congress with an explanation of the objections. If vetoed, Congress then has the power to vote the bill into law with two-thirds vote over presidential objections.

Another key control included by the authors of the Constitution is the judiciary. Even after a bill becomes law, it is not the final word. Dissenting parties can bring an action against the law and seek to have it brought before the judiciary. The highest court in the United States is the U.S. Supreme Court, consisting of nine jurists appointed by the president and confirmed by the Senate.

While the Constitution creates the judiciary, it leaves many structural details to the president and Congress. For example, the number of justices is decided through congressional legislation. Since 1869, the number has remained nine. Since 1869, there have been at least two discussions about changing the number of justices: (1) during President Franklin Delano Roosevelt's administration, and (2) after President Trump's appointments of three conservative justices, effectively shifting the balance that previously existed on the Court. Neither attempt succeeded, which some could argue demonstrates the effectiveness of the controls built into the Constitution.

Article III of the Constitution establishes the structure and function of the federal judiciary (see figure below). While the size of the Supreme Court is not settled in the Constitution, it is clearly identified as the highest court in the nation. As the court of last resort, the Supreme Court represents the last chance for individuals and groups to appeal decisions made by lower courts.

In addition, certain cases must be brought directly before the Supreme Court. These include cases involving:

1. Federal law and treaties,

2. Controversies between two or more states,

3. Controversies between federal and state governments,

4. Cases involving ambassadors, public ministers, consuls, and vice consuls,

5. Admiralty and maritime issues, and

6. A state and citizens of another state or foreign nation.

The judicial system, as the third branch of government, was established to balance the powers held by the legislative and executive branches by providing access to those with grievances over the exercise of those powers.

Table 2.2: Three Tiers of Judicial System

Top Tier: Supreme Court	Middle Tier: Courts of Appeals	Base Tier: District Courts
• This is the highest court and the final authority on federal law. • There is only one Supreme Court with nine justices.	• These courts review cases decided by the district courts below them. • There are 13 courts of appeals spread across 12 regional circuits and one special circuit for patent appeals. • Each court of appeals has a panel of judges that hear cases.	• These are the trial courts where evidence is presented and verdicts are reached. • There are 94 district courts spread throughout the country. • District courts can have jury trials and trials decided by a judge.

While we can infer from our reading of the U.S. Constitution and other associated writings of the Founding Fathers that administration was on their minds as they drafted the government's structure and scope, they did not specifically discuss it. The Constitution was born not during a time of peace but out of a period of rebellion, war, and civil and economic unrest. Given this context, expecting a perfect constitutional document to emerge would be unrealistic. Nevertheless, the founders produced a document that has survived and served the nation as it grew into maturity and world prominence.

Kettl (2018, p. 7) explains that the founders were so concerned with the abuse of administrative power that they did not specifically deal with administration in the Constitution. Instead, they focused on balancing the powers among the branches to prevent the abuses they feared most due to their experience under British rule. This left the forming of the government's administrative apparatus to those leaders occupying the offices established in the Constitution. This understanding leads to our next topic, explaining the origins and growth of the administrative structure of government in the United States.

STATUTORY ORIGINS OF FEDERAL EXECUTIVE-LEVEL AGENCIES

In 1887, Woodrow Wilson wrote that "policy does nothing without the aid of administration" (Wilson, 1887, p. 211). Congress being charged with passing laws and the president being responsible for running the government meant that an administrative apparatus was needed to effectively implement the laws passed by Congress and executed by the president. Wilson notes two important questions that needed to be answered: "what government can properly and successfully do" and "how [can it] do these proper things with the utmost possible efficiency and at the least possible cost either of money or energy" (1887, p. 197).

To address these challenges, Congress needed to pass "enabling legislation" (*The Law Dictionary*, n.d.)—laws creating the departments and agencies responsible for carrying out government policies. Article III, Section 8 of the Constitution states that Congress is responsible for making "all laws which shall be necessary and proper for carrying into execution the foregoing powers vested by this Constitution in the Government of the United States or in any department or officer thereof." The "foregoing powers" referenced the list of responsibilities assigned to Congress in the section leading up to that final statement.[1]

The exercise of this responsibility led to the creation of the first three executive-level agencies in 1789: (1) the Department of Foreign Affairs (renamed Department of State later that year), (2) the Department of Treasury, and (3) the Department of War (later renamed the Department of Defense[2]). In addition, Congress created the Office of the Attorney General, rounding out the first executive cabinet at four members.

The growth of the administrative functions in the United States progressed slowly over the first 90 years, from the adoption of the Constitution in 1789 until around 1880. Over the following 122 years, several major events or periods resulted in further growth in the government's administrative apparatus. These included the Industrial Revolution, World War I, the Great Depression, World War II, the Civil Rights Movement, and growing concerns over the environment and national security.

Over the course of U.S. history, some previously-created departments were merged or renamed. For example, the Department of War was later renamed the

---

1   Another issue that the U.S. government needed to deal with was the balance of powers between the federal government and the states, which resulted in the ratification of the Tenth Amendment (1791) to the Constitution. It states, "the powers not delegated to the United States by the Constitution, nor prohibited by it to the states, are reserved to the states respectively, or to the people." Even with this addition to the Constitution, conflicts over the exercise of power occur between the federal government and the various states.

2   National Security Act of 1947, in response to efforts by the United Nations to rebrand certain agencies around the world after World War II, renamed the Department of War as the Department of Defense.

Department of Defense, and the Office of the Attorney General was later merged into the Department of Justice.

Presently, there are four types of administrative departments or agencies: cabinet departments, independent executive agencies, regulatory agencies, and government corporations. The table that follows lists the cabinet-level departments and their years of creation. Cabinet agencies cover specific subject matter and employ individuals who develop expertise in those fields. The leaders of these departments are officials in the president's cabinet and advise the president on policies overseen by their agencies.

Table 2.3: List of Cabinet Level Agencies and Date of Creation

Year	Executive Department	Note
1789	Department of Foreign Affairs	Renamed Department of State in 1789
1789	Department of State*	
1789	Department of Treasury*	
1789	Department War	Renamed Department of Defense in 1947
1789	Attorney General	Merged with Department of Justice in 1870
1798	Department of the Navy	Merged with Department of Defense in 1947
1829	Postmaster General	Not on the President's Cabinet
1849	Department of the Interior*	
1862	Department of Agriculture*	
1870	Department of Justice*	Led by the Attorney General
1903	Department of Commerce and Labor	Later split into two separate agencies
1913	Department of Commerce*	
1913	Department of Labor*	
1947	Department of Defense*	Merged Departments of War and Navy
1953	Department of Health, Education, and Welfare	Later split into two separate agencies
1965	Department of Housing and Urban Development*	
1966	Department of Transportation*	
1977	Department of Energy*	
1979	Department of Education*	
1980	Department of Health & Human Services*	
1989	Department of Veterans Affairs*	
2002	Department of Homeland Security*	

*Denotes a member of the current president's cabinet (15 members).

In addition to the cabinet-level departments, there is a fluctuating number of independent executive agencies that are technically classified as part of the executive branch. According to a database maintained by the U.S. Office of

Personnel Management, over 100 independent agencies are presently operating. The chief distinctions between the cabinet-level departments (and their subdivisions) and independent agencies are their size and scope. Independent agencies are smaller and less complex in size and organization; their missions tend to be narrowly focused, unlike cabinet-level departments. They remain part of the executive branch but are not part of the cabinet. Examples of independent agencies include the National Aeronautics and Space Administration (NASA), the Central Intelligence Agency (CIA), and the National Science Foundation (NSF). See the table below for a current list retrieved on September 3, 2023.

There are two other sub-classifications of agencies in the federal system: regulatory agencies and government corporations. An example of a regulatory agency is the U.S. Environmental Protection Agency (EPA). An example of a government corporation is the U.S. Postal Service. Congress creates regulatory agencies to implement and enforce laws in such policy areas as public health, safety, the environment, and property. Government corporations, on the other hand, are established to provide market-based products and services. They are generally expected to generate sufficient revenues to cover their expenses and build appropriate reserves, like private corporations.

While our focus is on the federal government, state governments are organized in a similar way. The governor of each state has a cabinet consisting of agency or department heads who advise them on their respective policy areas. These departments were formed by similar enabling legislation passed by their respective policy areas.

The structures of local governments differ depending on their nature and jurisdiction, or scope. Most city governments are organized similarly to the state and federal governments, with a mayor and a council. Cities are governed by a charter and ordinances passed by the council and signed by the mayor. Counties, on the other hand, are administrative subdivisions of the state and often function with a commission and an executive overseeing the administrative apparatus.

Students wishing to learn more about local government can refer to the freely-available resources listed in the section on further reading.

THE ORIGIN, HISTORY, AND MISSION OF FEDERAL AGENCIES: A COMPARISON

Departments and agencies are created through enabling legislation passed by Congress and signed by the president. For example, let's examine the enabling legislation that led to the creation of the Department of Homeland Security. In the aftermath of the terrorist attacks on September 11, 2001, President George W. Bush issued Executive Order 13228 (October 8, 2001), establishing the Office of Homeland Security to coordinate responses to terrorist threats and attacks. Congress formalized this action by passing Public Law No. 107-296, or the Homeland Security Act of 2002, which took effect on November 25, 2002. Title I,

Section 101(a), states "there is established a Department of Homeland Security, as an executive department of the United States within the meaning of title 5, United States Code." Section 101(b)(1) outlines the mission of the new department.

A glaring problem that emerged during the investigation into the September 11 attacks was the fragmentation of the U.S. security umbrella. It became clear that too many different organizational units were attempting to secure the U.S. homeland, and coordinating intelligence-sharing and assessment of that intelligence into actionable information required too much political gamesmanship. These separate units often operated more like competitors than teammates.

The proposal to create a singular Department of Homeland Security aimed to address this issue by combining 22 individual departments and agencies under one official, and making it a cabinet-level department (see table 2.4 below).

Table 2.4: Agencies Merged into the Department of Homeland Security[3]

No.	Department/Agency Name
1	Transportation Security Administration
2	Coast Guard
3	Federal Emergency Management Agency
4	Secret Service
5	Customs and Border Protection
6	Immigration and Customs Enforcement
7	Citizenship and Immigration Services
8	Critical Infrastructure Assurance Office of the Department of Commerce
9	National Communications System of the Federal Bureau of Investigation (FBI)
10	National Infrastructure Simulation and Analysis Center
11	Energy Assurance Office of the Department of Energy
12	Federal Computer Incident Response Center of the General Services Administration
13	Federal Protective Service
14	Office of Domestic Preparedness
15	Federal Law Enforcement Training Center
16	Integrated Hazard Information System of the National Oceanic and Atmospheric Administration
17	National Domestic Preparedness Office of the FBI
18	Domestic Emergency Support Team of the Department of Justice
19	Metropolitan Medical Response System of the Department of Health and Human Services (DHHS)
20	National Disaster Medical System of the Department of Health and Human Services (DHHS)

---

3 Prepared using information obtained from several websites including Why the Department of Homeland Security Was Created (thoughtco.com)

No.	Department/Agency Name
21	Office of Emergency Preparedness and the Strategic National Stockpile of DHHS
22	Plum Island Animal Disease Center of the Department of Agriculture

The challenge with creating a single department by combining so many individual organizational units is that each had its own culture and operating environment. All of these units had to adapt to a new reality: operating under a unified mission. That mission has evolved since DHS's first year of operation. The current mission statement, obtained directly from the DHS website, is: "With honor and integrity, we will safeguard the American people, our homeland, and our values." At the time of its birth, the DHS was considered a high-risk agency because of the challenges involved in merging and assimilating so many different units into one department structure with a singular mission.[4] However, as noted on the same site, DHS has made significant progress in address the Government Accountability Office's concerns.

A second example is the origin of the Department of Environmental Protection (EPA). While the Department of Homeland Security (DHS) is a cabinet-level agency, the EPA is a regulatory agency and not part of the president's cabinet. The origin of this agency is interesting. We start with a quote from *Silent Spring* by Rachel Carson (1962): "but man is a part of nature, and his war against nature is inevitably a war against himself" (p. 6). While the connection between the book and President Nixon's endeavor to promote and support a federal environmental policy is unclear, it is referenced on the EPA's own webpage and was part of President Kennedy's reading list. Regardless of whether President Nixon read the book, the environmental activism movement that emerged in the late 1950s directly led to the first major piece of environmental legislation passed by Congress and signed into law by a president who did not particularly respect environmental activism.

Congress passed the first major law establishing a comprehensive environmental policy in 1969, titled National Environmental Policy Act. In July of 1970, President Nixon made a special address to Congress in advance of signing the bill into law. The EPA's first official day of operation was December 2, 1970, although the agency was conceived earlier that year. President Nixon signed two executive orders—Reorganization Plan No. 3 and Reorganization Plan No. 4. Plan No. 3 created the Department of Environmental Protection (EPA), and Plan No. 4 created the National Oceanic and Atmospheric Administration (NOAA).

The formation of the EPA, like DHS, consolidated a variety of already-existing government units under one agency charged with overseeing environmental regulation in the United States. This pattern often recurs with agency formation: the birth of a new entity is often preceded by problems that a fragmented approach failed to address.

To make the formation of the new agency official, Congress held committee meetings with final votes at the committee level. In the House, the Government

---

4   https://www.dhs.gov/gao-high-risk-management

Operations Subcommittee on Executive and Legislative Reorganization held hearings and approved the executive orders, while in the Senate, the Government Operations Subcommittee on Executive Reorganization and Government Research did the same. Before the vote, Congress debated whether the agency should be an independent regulatory agency or a cabinet-level agency. In the end, they agreed with the president's proposal and voted the new independent regulatory agency into existence.

The mission of the EPA begins with a simple opening statement, "To protect human health and the environment." This is followed by a series of objectives focusing on specific policy areas, including clean air, clean water, clean land, stewardship, and chemical safety. The agency is organized into twelve offices (administrative, oversight, and regulatory), and ten regions. The country is divided into ten regions, each with its own office organized similarly to the headquarters in Washington, D.C.

The operational offices include the Office of Air and Radiation, Office of Chemical Safety and Pollution Prevention, Office of Water, Office of Land and Emergency Management, Office of International and Tribal Affairs, Office of Environmental Justice and External Civil Rights, Office of Enforcement and Compliance Assurance, Office of Mission Support, and Office of Research and Development. Administrative offices include the Office of the Chief Financial Officer, Office of General Counsel, and Office of Inspector General.

Each operational office has its own charge. For example, the Office of Water exists to protect the nation's drinking water supply and is also charged with restoring and maintaining the oceans, watersheds, and their aquatic ecosystems. Its focus includes protecting human health, the economy, and the nation's natural resources, such as fish, plants, and wildlife habitats. The Office of Water is further divided into the Office of the Assistant Administrator for Water, the Office of Ground Water and Drinking Water, the Office of Science and Technology, the Office of Wastewater Management, and the Office of Wetlands, Oceans, and Watersheds.

While headquartered in Washington, D.C., the Office of Water also maintains offices in each of the ten regions. Major programs administered through this office include the Clean Water Act and the Safe Drinking Water Act.

THE ROLE OF CONGRESSIONAL OVERSIGHT OF FEDERAL EXECUTIVE AGENCIES

A good follow-up question to ask is: How do elected leaders maintain oversight of all these agencies and departments? A report by the Congressional Research Service (CRS), last updated on December 13, 2022, begins with the statement, "Congress engages in oversight of the executive branch through the review, monitoring, and supervision of the implementation of public policy." The power of Congress to perform oversight is not explicitly stated in the Constitution but has been the subject of a series of Supreme Court cases. Oversight and investigations generally occur within congressional committees.

The CRS report lists three major purposes of oversight: programmatic, political, and institutional. This discussion focuses on programmatic oversight, which, according to the CRS, ensures that "agencies and programs are working in a cost-effective and efficient manner and fulfilling their statutory mission." Programmatic oversight may include investigations into (1) compliance with legislative intent, (2) program performance, (3) fraud, waste, and abuse, (4) the rulemaking process, (5) and general information gathering for future policymaking.

In addition to congressional oversight and investigation, there are at least two other formal means of providing appropriate oversight with investigative potential. The first is the system of inspectors general (IGs) operating throughout federal departments and agencies (CRS, 2021, 2023b). The second is the independent oversight agency, the Government Accountability Office (GAO) (CRS, 2021). While both serve similar functions, they differ in origin, placement, and operation. Oversight performed by both GAO and agency IGs informs Congress and provides valuable information that may be used in congressional oversight activities.

The role of inspector general is relatively new compared to the Constitution. The first IG was appointed in 1959 within the Department of State. The role within cabinet and independent agencies was formalized in 1978 with the passage of the Inspector General Act. Since then, additional legislation has enhanced the independence of the office and expanded staff access to records needed for completing their assignments. The IG performs various assignments, including performance audits, inspections, evaluations, and investigations, listed here in order of their scope.

The operations of IGs are governed by professional standards, such as: the Yellow Book for audits, the Blue Book for inspections and evaluations, and Quality Standards for Investigations.

The Government Accountability Office was established in 1921 with the passage of the Budget and Accounting Act. Originally named the General Accounting Office, the agency was renamed in 2004 to reflect its evolving role in federal governance. While initially focused on financial audits, the GAO later included performance audits focusing on efficiency, effectiveness, economy, and compliance. The agency also has a branch dedicated to conducting criminal investigations.

The GAO employs a large workforce with a broad range of specialties reflecting the agency's broad scope of activities. Its mission statement declares: "We support Congress in meeting its constitutional responsibilities and help improve performance and ensure the accountability of the federal government. We provide Congress with timely information that is objective, fact-based, non-partisan, non-ideological, and balanced."

Up to this point in your reading, it should be clear that public service offers opportunities for individuals with diverse backgrounds. Whether your interests are in operations, policy, or oversight, there is a place for you in public service.

The next and final section of this chapter will briefly address public service opportunities available to those seeking careers in the public sector. The important takeaway thus far is that government needs an effective administrative apparatus to function. This need was envisioned by the framers of the Constitution and has been upheld by those who occupy elected seats of power at all levels of government. Without administration, the government would grind to a halt, unable to meet the needs of its citizens and other stakeholders.

CAREERS IN PUBLIC SERVICE

Why do people choose to work in government rather than in the private sector? This is a question academics have been exploring for quite some time. Perry and Wise (1990) define public service motivation as: "an individual's predisposition to respond to motives grounded primarily or uniquely in public institutions or organizations." Put simply, some people are drawn to work in organizations whose role is to eliminate deficiencies identified in society—whether they are social, economic, political, or environmental.

People may seek opportunities in the public sector for pragmatic reasons, such as work-life balance and job security. Others may identify with a specific program or policy area and wish to work to further its advancement. Others may be motivated by a desire to serve the needs of others without the pressures of profit-driven work. Whatever the reason, the public sector offers abundant opportunities.

So far, we have focused on the federal government, and we will continue that focus while also discussing how to identify opportunities at the state and local levels. At the federal level, there are two paths into public service: appointed positions and those obtained through the civil service process (Ingraham, 1995).

There are three levels of executive and policy-sensitive positions appointed by the president: (1) heads of departments and agencies, who are generally appointed by the president and approved by the Senate; (2) senior executive service members, who are appointed by the president; and (3) policy-sensitive positions, or Schedule-C positions, which are also appointed by the president. Most other positions are hired through the civil service process.

Those working in government may serve in traditional business administration roles, such as human resources, facilities and maintenance, accounting and finance, or information technology. Others may work in particular program or policy offices, developing expertise in a specific area. Some employers will interact with citizens accessing government services, while others will perform regulatory duties or work in activities protecting national security.

The point is, there are many paths one can take in public service. But how does one go about researching opportunities in government?

At the federal level, there is a centralized personnel function designed to communicate available opportunities across all the branches and organizational units of the federal government. To identify career opportunities, individuals can visit usajobs.gov, create a profile, search for open positions, and apply. The website includes information about working for the federal government, the hiring process, and those positions identified as urgent needs. Applicants upload their resumes and make them searchable, so federal government talent recruiters may identify specific candidates of interest. The website also has options to explore the various hiring paths, such as programs for individuals with disabilities, Native Americans, or military spouses. This website can serve as your only access point for the federal employment portal.

Individuals seeking federal employment should also visit the websites of the departments and agencies they most want to work for in order to learn more about them.

Additional information about federal employment is available through the Office of Personnel Management (OPM) at opm.gov. The OPM site links to usajobs.gov but also includes other information, such as information about the different levels within the federal service, including senior executive service and civil service. The site provides details on salaries, benefits, labor relations, and other information of interest to job seekers. Additionally, it contains information needed by departments and agencies wishing to post vacant positions.

Like the federal system, states have their own department or agency similar to the Office of Personnel Management. For example, individuals interested in state employment in Georgia can visit careers.georgia.gov to research available opportunities. This site functions similarly to usajobs.gov. Counties and other local governments also operate their own websites to advertise open positions and facilitate applications.

It is important to keep in mind that the public sector environment can vary depending on where you live in the United States. For example, in some southern states, which are right-to-work states, unions tend to be weak. In contrast, northern states tend to have much stronger unions, and the hiring process can involve taking civil service exams to qualify for further consideration.

CONCLUSION

After reading this chapter, one should develop an understanding and appreciation of the scope and depth of government operations. While not specifically set out in the Constitution, the framers gave thought to and included hints about the existence of the administrative apparatus necessary to ensure the freedoms and liberties intended for citizens.

The function and structure of this administrative apparatus was left to elected officials—namely, the president and Congress. Through a process requiring negotiation, these leaders at first constructed the government slowly, but over time, it developed more rapidly into the government we see in operation today.

Is the administrative apparatus really a "fourth branch" of government? This is still a question open to debate. However, there is no doubt that government relies on it to accomplish the work necessary to run a nation like the United States.

REFERENCES

Congressional Research Services (CRS). (2021, April 12). *GAO and inspector general recommendations to agencies: An introduction* (Report No. IF11807). Retrieved September 7, 2023, from https://crsreports.congress.gov/product/pdf/IF/IF11807

Congressional Research Services (CRS). (2022, December 13). *Congressional oversight and investigations* (Report No. IFI0015). Retrieved September 3, 2023, from https://crsreports.congress.gov/product/pdf/IF/IF10015

Congressional Research Services (CRS). (2023, January 12). *An introduction to oversight of offices of inspector general* (Report No. IF11869). Retrieved September 7, 2023, from https://crsreports.congress.gov/product/pdf/IF/IF11869

Congressional Research Services (CRS). (2023, February 8). *Statutory inspectors general in the federal government: A primer* (Report No. R45450). Retrieved September 3, 2023, from https://crsreports.congress.gov/product/pdf/R/R45450

Crews, C. W., Jr. (2017, July 5). How many federal agencies exist? We can't drain the swamp until we know. *Forbes*. Retrieved July 25, 2023, from https://www.forbes.com/sites/waynecrews/2017/07/05/how-many-federal-agencies-exist-we-cant-drain-the-swamp-until-we-know/?sh=578feb6a1aa2

Exec. Order No. 13228, 3 C.F.R. 795 (2001). U.S. Government Printing Office. https://www.govinfo.gov/content/pkg/WCPD-2001-10-15/pdf/WCPD-2001-10-15-Pg1434.pdf

Homeland Security Act of 2002, H.R. 5005, 107th Congress (2002, November 25). https://www.congress.gov/bill/107th-congress/house-bill/5005/text

Kettl, D. F. (2018). *Politics of the administrative process*. CQ Press.

Library of Congress. (n.d.). *Legal research: A guide to administrative law, rules and rulemaking*. Retrieved September 1, 2023, from https://guides.loc.gov/administrative-law/rules

Madison, J. (2012). Federalist 51, the structure of the government must furnish the proper checks and balances between the different departments. In *The constitution of the United States of America and selected writings of the founding fathers* (pp. 484–488). Barnes and Noble, Inc.

The Law Dictionary. (n.d.). Enabling clause. In *The law dictionary featuring Black's law dictionary* (2nd ed.). Retrieved September 1, 2023, from https://thelawdictionary.org/enabling-clause

The White House a. (n.d.). *The executive branch*. Retrieved July 25, 2023, from https://www.whitehouse.gov/about-the-white-house/our-government/the-executive-branch/

The White House b. (n.d.). *The legislative branch*. Retrieved July 25, 2023, from https://www.whitehouse.gov/about-the-white-house/our-government/the-legislative-branch/

The White House c. (n.d.). *The judicial branch*. Retrieved July 25, 2023, from https://

www.whitehouse.gov/about-the-white-house/our-government/the-judicial-branch/

U.S. Department of State (n.d.). *Administrative timeline of the department of state.* Retrieved September 1, 2023, from https://history.state.gov/departmenthistory/timeline/1789-1899

U.S. Department of State (n.d.). *A history of the United States department of state 1789-1996.* Retrieved September 1, 2023, from https://1997-2001.state.gov/about_state/history/dephis.html

U.S. Office of Personnel Management. (n.d.). *Executive branch civilian employment since 1940.* Retrieved July 25, 2023, from https://www.opm.gov/policy-data-oversight/data-analysis-documentation/federal-employment-reports/historical-tables/

U.S. Office of Personnel Management. (n.d.). *Open government data, federal agencies list.* Retrieved September 2, 2023, from https://www.opm.gov/about-us/open-government/Data/Apps/Agencies/index.aspx

U.S. v. Germaine, 99 U.S. 508 (1878). https://www.law.cornell.edu/supremecourt/text/99/508

U.S. Constitution, Preamble.

Wilson, W. (1887). The study of administration. *Political Science Quarterly*, 2(2), 197–222.

Paradigms of Public Administration

LEARNING OBJECTIVES

Students studying this chapter should be able to:

1. Describe the early development of public administration in the United States.
2. Distinguish between the five major paradigms of public administration theory.
3. Discuss how these paradigms have changed the practice of public administration.
4. Explain views on the future of public administration in the 21st Century.

INTRODUCTION

Public administration in the United States is an evolving field. The nature of the administrative state changed as the nation matured and grew in both physical size and population. The intellectual history of public administration is usually divided into five periods or paradigms (Henry, 1975) beginning in the 1880s with Woodrow Wilson's seminal paper (Wilson, 1887). However, the history of the field predates that paper, beginning with the reform of the civil service system and the Pendleton Act of 1883 (Rosenbloom, 2008). Knowing the intellectual history of the field helps to place its present state within a historical context.

The field of public administration has been shaped through the nation's fragile beginnings, a bloody five-year Civil War, the late 19th-century Industrial Revolution, a growing national population, and the shift from a rural to an increasingly urban population, along with two world wars. The field has been further impacted by the development of technology and the information age. These more recent developments continue to influence the field. What will public administration look like by the end of the 21st Century?

PRE-1800'S: THE EARLY YEARS

The Constitution, written by the founders, presented the basic framework for running the government; however, as with any new system, the initial implementation was rarely without challenges. Changes were often needed in response to issues that arose over time. The early period of public administration is a story of firsts: the first president, the first Congress, the first executive cabinet, the first laws, and the first regulations. As a basic framework, the Constitution was not a complete model for the new government. Many details were left to the first generation of leaders to figure out, and they were acutely aware of that responsibility. Early experiences and challenges thus played a key role in the development of public administration.

One example of the challenges the new government faced was the Whiskey Rebellion in Pennsylvania and Ohio (1791–1794), which internally tested the federal government's ability to enforce law and maintain unity (Kohn, 1972). Another challenge was the War of 1812 with the British, which firmly established the United States as a nation capable of defending itself against outside aggressors (National Park Service, n.d.). These challenges tested the new government's ability to respond to and protect the young nation from both internal and external threats.

George Washington, serving as the nation's first president, faced several challenges by being the first to occupy the office. He had to learn how to be president while developing a "presidential" leadership style and defining the inner workings of the presidency. Washington also needed to collect information on public opinion and manage the new executive cabinet. President Washington understood the fragile nature of the new nation, an understanding apparent in how some of his contemporaries described his style as thoughtful and deliberate (Cook & Klay, 2015). As a decision-maker, he sought information from many sources before making final decisions. This deliberation attested to his awareness of the importance of being the first to serve as president and setting precedents for future administrations to follow. Among these precedents, he focused on developing a professional public administration that valued education and expertise and committed to defining public administration as a trust between the government and those it represented.

In his farewell address, Washington reminded the nation about the importance of focusing on shared values rather than on the differences that were sure to emerge as the nation grew and matured (Washington, 1796). He focused on three challenges facing the new nation. First, Washington warned of regional threats, where different geographic regions might focus on their own interests rather than the nation's best interests. Second, he warned against partisan factionalism due to allegiances to parties or individuals over the collective interests of the nation. Lastly, he warned of external threats stemming from foreign entanglements.

Frederick Mosher describes these early years of public administration as "government by gentlemen" (Ingraham, 1995, p. 17). During the first 40 years of the nation's history, government was dominated by landed gentlemen. The right to vote—and, consequently, a prerequisite to government service—was restricted to those holding a certain station in society. Voting rights were limited to landholding men, and the first public servants emerged exclusively from that group.

The election of Andrew Jackson as president in 1828 marked the beginning of the "Spoils Era" (Ingraham, 1995, p. 20). Spoils refers to the practice of rewarding government jobs as political rewards for supporting candidates. During this era, the political process and access to government jobs were extended to the "common" men of the nation. Reform of the spoils system began after a disgruntled political supporter assassinated President James Garfield. In response, Congress passed, and President Chester A. Arthur signed, the Pendleton Act of 1883, which created the merit-based civil service system.

The end of the nation's first 100 years also marked an increase in government regulation. The Sherman Antitrust Act, passed in 1890, signaled the beginning of a new period in which the government sought to regulate businesses to protect the public from business behaviors labelled as anti-competitive (Vogel, 2017).

1887 TO 1926: BRIGHT LINE BETWEEN POLITICS AND ADMINISTRATION

Scholars and researchers often view the Reform Movement that began in the 1880s as the birth of public administration as an academic discipline in the United States. For example, in 1887, Woodrow Wilson published "The Study of Administration" focusing on administration as a science (Wilson, 1887). Later, in 1900, academic Frank J. Goodnow published his book *Politics and Administration* (2005), where he wrote about the two functions of government: the expression of the will of the state and the discharge of that will (p. 22). Wilson's writing focused on the importance of separating partisan politics from professional administration, while Goodnow wrote about the need to recognize political parties as an official organ of politics. Goodnow appears to conclude that incorporating political parties as an official organ was essential for efficient administration (pp. 255–263).

Woodrow Wilson (1887) extended the idea of reform beyond civil service to encompass all administrative functions. He believed that the Constitution did not dictate administration but instead equated public administration with business. Wilson distinguished between the academic fields of political science and public administration, viewing politics as the process of establishing law and policy and administration as the execution of those laws and policies. He emphasized that in executing law and policy, administration must consider public opinion. He also asserted that administration extends to, and has administrative principles transferable to, all levels of government.

Frank J. Goodnow (1900), on the other hand, saw a merit-based administration as compatible with democracy, because not administration but democracy defines the political system. He argued that administration is a science to be learned and practiced by trained professionals who should take on the role of executing policies effectively and efficiently. Both Goodnow and Wilson wrote of the "will of the state," with politics establishing that will and administration carrying it out.

1927 TO 1937: DEVELOPING ADMINISTRATIVE PRINCIPLES

The Industrial Revolution brought both benefits and challenges to society. This period witnessed the rise of the corporation as a dominant form of business. Large corporations, employing new scientific principles of production and management, employed large numbers of people. However, the shift from a rural, agriculture- and crafts-focused population to an urban one with a more centralized industrial economy also ushered in an increasing number of social, economic, and political problems. This shift increased the importance of effective management and organizational leadership.

Three key individuals associated with the birth of classical management theory are Max Weber, Frederick Taylor, and Henri Fayol. Weber's writings, translated into English in the 1920s, focused on bureaucracy. Nickerson (2024) identifies five criteria composing Weber's organizational theory: (1) hierarchical structure, (2) management by rules, (3) organization by function, (4) impersonality, and (5) individual's technical qualifications. Frederick W. Taylor, in his January 25, 1912 testimony to Congress, described four basic principles of the science of management: studying the work to be done, selecting workers, merging selected workers with the science of the work, and equitably dividing labor between workers and management. Taylor's scientific principles complemented the ideas put forth by public administration reformers advocating for public administration as a science. Fayol's contributions to management literature included defining five functions and fourteen principles of management, which remain relevant today. We examine these functions and principles in greater detail in chapter eight.

Administrative reforms also extended to state and local levels of government. For example, in *The Movement of Budgetary Reform in the United States*, William F. Willoughby wrote about the use of the budget as a mechanism linking politics and administration (Willoughby, 1918). Additionally, new forms of local government appeared that incorporated a professional manager or administrator to oversee the business affairs of local government (Burns, 1994).

In 1937, Luther Gulick published "Notes on the Theory of Organization," addressing principles for managing organizations. That same year, he and Lyndall Urwick also published *Papers on the Science of Administration*, introducing the mnemonic POSDCORB (planning, organizing, staffing, directing, coordinating, reporting, and budgeting) into the study of management (Gulick & Urwick, 1937). These seven activities were identified as the core set of functions performed by management within an organization.

Gulick also worked with Louis Brownlow and Charles Merriam to produce the *Report of the President's Committee on Administrative Management* in

1937 (Shafritz et al., 2004, p. 99). President Franklin D. Roosevelt had appointed the committee to study and suggest a reorganization of the executive branch in response to the significant increase in the number of agencies created during the New Deal era.

1938 TO 1947: CHALLENGING THE EXISTING PARADIGMS

The more mechanistic view of management and administration that emerged with the development of public administration as a science, the scientific method, and classical management theory was challenged by the Human Relations Theory. Key contributions to this school of thought include Elton Mayo's studies at a Western Electric plant from 1924 to 1932, which demonstrated the importance of communication between management and employees; Herbert Simon's work on decision-making; Chester Barnard's writings on informal and formal organizations (Shafritz et al., 2004, p. 104); Abraham Maslow's writings on motivation theory; and Douglas McGregor's Theory X and Theory Y.

Human Relations Theory focused on interactions between people in the work environment. It shifted the focus from tasks and activities toward trying to understand why people behave as they do and identifying the factors that influence or drive behavior. The chief contribution of Human Relations Theory was its focusing on the behavioral aspects of management over a more technical approach to studying it.

1948 TO 1970: STRUGGLE FOR AN IDENTITY

Early signs of a struggle for the identity of public administration showed up as early as 1945 with Paul Appleby's book *Big Democracy*. Appleby identifies three complementary aspects that differentiate government from other organizations:

1. Breadth of scope, impact, and consideration

2. Public accountability

3. Political character

Questions about orthodoxy and the politics/administration dichotomy were addressed by Dwight Waldo in *The Administrative State*, published in 1948. Waldo speculates on whether the orthodox theory of public administration would remain the dominant theory or if something new might come along in the future to challenge it. Seeking to foster a discussion about the future of public administration, Waldo hosted a meeting of young public administration scholars in 1968, after joining the faculty at Syracuse University's Maxwell School. Known as Minnowbrook, after its location in upstate New York, this conference has been held every 20 years since 1968 to advance the discussion of public administration.

1971 TO PRESENT: BREAKTHROUGHS—NEW PUBLIC ADMINISTRATION (NPA)

The Minnowbrook Conference brought young scholars in public administration together at one location to discuss public administration (Nabatchi & Carboni, 2019). The conference resulted in the introduction of fresh, new thoughts on the field, including many that challenged the foundational principles of orthodoxy that had been in place since the early 20th century. A new framework was coined, "New Public Administration."

H. George Frederickson (1971) wrote about the New Public Administration framework that arose from Minnowbrook (Shafritz et al., 2004, p. 315). The orthodox view of public administration focused on providing services to the public as effectively, efficiently, and economically as possible, as previously stated. This view emphasized institutions rather than people. Human Relations theorists turned their attention to the relationship between managers and workers but still prioritized decision-making processes. The New Public Administration, however, shifted the focus to achieving social equity through change.

The New Public Administration (NPA) refuted the idea of a clear division between politics and administration. Instead, the NPA reasoned that policy was inherently a part of administration. It viewed administrators not as neutral implementers of law but as active participants in shaping policies to ensure they protected the interests of the most vulnerable (Guy & McCandless, 2012). Frederickson used the example of the Department of Agriculture: while the agency's focus was on farmers, some policies it implemented could harm farm workers and consumers. According to Frederickson, the job of administrators was to implement laws in such a way that they protect other less-powerful groups from being harmed by policy. This new school of thought represented a radical shift in the perceived role of administrators and rejected the idea of a clear boundary between politics and administration.

Not long after the arrival of NPA, an opposing or alternate view of public administration surfaced. Calls to adopt New Public Management began appearing in the 1980s. The election of Ronald Reagan as president ushered in a period of hostility toward government, which was viewed as an overbearing landlord extracting rents from citizens and businesses while living high on the hog. The government was deemed inefficient and incapable of delivering services effectively. Policymakers and administrators were criticized for lacking a focus on the economical use of resources, and the government was seen as wasteful and out of touch with the people it was meant to serve.

1971 TO PRESENT: BREAKTHROUGHS—NEW PUBLIC MANAGEMENT (NPM)

New Public Management (NPM), perhaps best exemplified in the writings of Osborne and Gaebler during the 1990s, emphasized making government operate more like a business (Osborne & Gaebler, 1992). The author of this unit suggests that the rise of NPM was, in part, a reaction to New Public Administration's (NPA) focus on social equity. This period also marked the beginning of significant challenges in the U.S. concerning civil discourse and cooperation among people. Problems increasingly came to be viewed in stark black-and-white terms, leaving little room for compromise or gray areas. This shift fueled heated debates and conflict, which began to adopt a winner-take-all mentality—a trend that has only grown more pronounced in contemporary political, economic, and social discourse.

NPM's key themes include control, value, and efficiency (Hood, 1995). Social equity has little room in a framework that focuses almost exclusively on measuring and proving the value of every dollar raised and spent at all levels of government. Performance measurement has become a dominant practice, with the underlying assumption that if programs and activities cannot be justified through documented and measurable performance metrics, they may not be worth pursuing. This approach led to an increased emphasis on privatizing government programs and activities, based on the argument that the private sector could deliver services to the public more efficiently and economically. NPM also introduced terms like "entrepreneurial" and "innovative" into the vocabulary of public administration.

21ST CENTURY AND BEYOND: NEW DIRECTIONS?

The beginning of the 21st century introduced a new framework referred to as New Public Service (Denhardt & Denhardt, 2000; 2015). New Public Service (NPS) differs markedly from New Public Management (NPM). Rather than emphasizing a business mindset, NPS centers on the political process, focusing on citizens, the public interest, and serving those interests through coalition building. Whether this will be the dominant framework for the 21st century remains uncertain—only time will tell.

Where we go from here is still open to discussion and debate. A few observations might help focus the discussion on what comes next, particularly regarding the effects of advancing technology. For example, technology is shrinking the world, speeding up processes, replacing the legacy manual paper-based processes with new cloud-based systems, increasing the need for advanced technical training among administrators, and increasing the focus on security.

Clearly, the technological advancement is fundamentally changing our lives. All of our data is now stored in places we can neither see nor visit. We access this data, and process transactions from our desks, computers, or devices. We are connected to the world from the comfort of our couch, bed, or office chair. Information is accessible to us more quickly than ever before, with access changing to live, instantaneous updates.

Artificial intelligence (AI) is aiding us in making decisions and is going to become an extension of our own minds. When we need answers, we will simply ask our phones, tablets, or computers or offices—and receive responses almost instantly. However, technology has both a bright and dark side. While it connects us and frees us from physical limitations, it also leaves us vulnerable, as access becomes harder to control.

Data is increasingly exposed to potential theft and manipulation. Software and data systems are accessible to outsiders set on penetrating our most elaborate protections. Unfortunately, they are often successful in these nefarious activities. Both private and public organizations face hostage situations where outsiders steal data, take control of hardware, or capture internal applications (such as email systems), demanding payment for their return or release.

Identity theft is also on the rise. Few people in the modern world—aside from those in areas still untouched by technology—are exempt from this risk. Electronic business-to-business and business-to-customer processes are replacing face-to-face transactions, further exposing us to vulnerabilities. These risks leave those responsible for data security restless and, often, sleepless at night.

It is doubtful that any of the past paradigms have prepared us adequately for the new challenges and threats we face today and will face in the future. We have entered a new information or digital age. Life moves fast, and administrators must be able to keep pace. This will be a significant challenge for all future administrators.

At a minimum, the field of public administration must keep up with societal changes. Ideally, it should be ahead of the curve, thinking ahead and addressing changes rather than reacting and struggling to catch up. The key term for the future of public administration is governance.

Attention is shifting away from traditional organizations and institutions toward processes, technology, and people. Students reading this textbook may become the future scholars who will be challenged to seek a new paradigm that appropriately addresses the evolving context in which we live and work. That is the challenge.

CONCLUSION

This textbook introduces many students to what is likely their first course in public administration. The authors hope that by the end of their study, students will develop a new appreciation for the role of the public administrator in modern society. Students should keep an open mind as they explore the material presented. No subject is wasted—every course on every subject contributes to the ability to think more clearly, strategically, and critically as well as discriminating in their choice of options. Observing and processing information quickly will be critical, as will avoiding significant missteps.

This section has taken readers on a journey through time—from the founding of a new nation, through its adolescence, and into its adulthood. Now, as a mature nation, it faces challenging situations, dangerous threats, and limitless opportunities. One thing, however, remains constant: the importance of public administrators being professional. This means being well-rounded, thoughtful, deliberate, and capable decision-makers.

This professional ideal harkens back to the 1800s and the introduction of the politics-administration dichotomy. It is important for students to understand that this dichotomy does not mean that administration is or should be free of politics. Rather, it refers to the mitigation of partisan or party politics in administration (Rosenbloom, 2008). Politics is an integral part of administration, just as administration is an integral part of politics. Think of it as a Reese's Peanut Butter Cup—you can't have one without the other; the chocolate and peanut butter must work together.

REFERENCES

Burns, N. (1994). *The formation of American local governments: Private values in public institutions*. New York, NY: Oxford University Press.

Cook, S. A., & Klay, W. E. (2015). George Washington's precedents: The institutional legacy of the American republic's founding public administrator. *Administration and Society, 47*(1), 75-95.

Denhardt, R. B., & Denhardt, J. V. (2000). The new public service: Serving rather than steering. *Public Administration Review, 60*(6), 549–559. http://www.jstor.org/stable/977437

Denhardt, J. V., & Denhardt, R. B. (2015). The new public service revisited. *Public Administration Review, 75*(5), 664–672. http://www.jstor.org/stable/24757439

Goodnow, F. J. (2005). *Politics and administration*. Brunswick, NJ: Transaction Publishers.

Gulick, L. H., & Urwick, L. F. (1937). *Papers on the science of administration*. A.M. Kelly.

Gulick, L. (1937). *Notes on the theory of organization*. New York, NY: Columbia University, Institute of Public Administration.

Guy, M. E., & McCandless, S. A. (2012). Social equity: Its legacy, its promise. *Public Administration Review, 72*, S5–S13. http://www.jstor.org/stable/41688032

Henry, N. (1975). Paradigms of public administration. *Public Administration Review, 35*(4), 378–386. https://doi.org/10.2307/974540

Hood, C. (1995). The "new public management" in the 1980's: Variations on a theme. *Accounting, Organizations, and Society, 20*(2–3), 93–109, https://doi.org/10.1016/0361-3682(93)W0001-W

Ingraham, P. W. (1995). *The foundation of merit: Public service in American democracy*. Baltimore, MD: The Johns Hopkins University Press.

Kohn, R. H. (1972). The Washington administration's decision to crush the whiskey rebellion. *The Journal of American History, 59*(3), 567–584. https://doi.org/10.2307/1900658

Nabatchi, T., & Carboni, J. L. (2019). *Assessing the past and future of public administration: Reflections from the Minnowbrook at 50 conference*. Maxwell School of Citizenship and Public Affairs, Syracuse University.

National Park Service (n.d.). *Star spangled banner: History and culture.* https://www.nps.gov/stsp/learn/historyculture/index.htm

Nickerson, C. (2024). Bureaucratic management theory of Max Weber. *Simply Psychology.* https://simplypsychology.org/bureaucratic-theory-weber.html

O'Leary, R. (2011). Minnowbrook: Tradition, idea, spirit, event, challenge. *Journal of Public Administration Research and Theory, 21*(i1–i6), http://www.jstor.org/stable/40961913

Osborne, D., & Gaebler, T. (1992). *Reinventing government: How the entrepreneurial spirit is transforming the public sector from school house to statehouse, to city hall to the Pentagon.* Reading, MA: Addison-Wesley.

Osborne, D. (1993). Reinventing government. *Public Productivity & Management Review, 16*(4), 349–356. https://doi.org/10.2307/3381012

Pollitt, C. (1995). Justification by works or by faith? Evaluating the new public management. *Evaluation, 1*(2), 133–154. https://doi.org/10.1177/135638909500100202

Rosenbloom, D. (2008). The politics-administration dichotomy in U.S. historical context. *Public Administration Review, 68*(1), 57–60. http://www.jstor.org/stable/25145576

Schuyler, M. (2014). *Fiscal fact no. 415: A short history of government taxing and spending in the United States.* Washington, DC: Tax Foundation.

Shafritz, J. M., & Hyde, A. C. (2004). *Classics of public administration* (5th ed.). Belmont, CA: Wadsworth, Cengage Learning.

Shafritz, J. M. (2004). *The dictionary of public policy and administration.* Boulder, CO: Westview Press.

Washington, G. (1796) Farewell address to the people of the United States, announcing his intention of retiring from public life at the expiration of the present constitutional term of presidency. *Zea E-Books in American Studies.* 31. https://digitalcommons.unl.edu/zeaamericanstudies/31

Willoughby, W. F. (1918) *The movement for budgetary reform in the states.* New York, NY: D. Appleton and Company.

Wilson, W. (1887). The study of administration. *Political Science Quarterly, 2*(2), 197–222.

Public Sector Decision-Making

LEARNING OBJECTIVES

Students studying this unit should be able to:

1. Describe the decision-making process in the public sector.
2. Identify the challenges faced in decision-making within public administration.
3. Discuss the methods used to ensure compliance with policies and decisions.
4. Explain the key issues in addressing the evaluation of policy and decision outcomes.

INTRODUCTION

The previous chapter addressed organizational theories that influence the structure of the American government. This chapter shifts the focus to the role of decision-making in government. Imagine yourself as a public administrator faced with a pandemic like the one in 2020. In such a scenario, everyone looks to you for information, leadership, and a plan. Decision-making becomes critical during periods of crisis but remains a crucial activity even in more normal times and circumstances. Knowing how to make decisions, when to make them, and how to assess them lies at the heart of public administration. As noted earlier in the text, public administration theory has evolved through several periods or paradigms, and decision-making theory has evolved alongside it.

This chapter will introduce the various schools of thought on decision-making and highlights individual theoretical contributions. While academic in nature, these theories reflect actual practices, making them useful to learn. Equally important are the constraints on decision-making, including the administrative controls within organizations. This chapter also discusses performance measurement, a key aspect for public administrators to determine how their decisions are evaluated after implementation. The primary question usually focuses on impact: were the goals and objectives achieved? Finally, the decision-making theories presented are not limited to public administration; they are equally applicable to public, nonprofit, and private organizations.

HOW ARE DECISIONS MADE?

The public administration literature identifies three basic decision-making models: classical, administrative, and retrospective. The classical model describes decision-making as a systematic, step-by-step, rational process. A sound decision is achieved by carefully fulfilling each step, leading to the best or optimal decision. Its systematic and structured approach makes it straightforward to learn, follow, and apply.

The classical model is based on a set of fundamental assumptions. It requires that problems and objectives are clearly defined, all alternatives are known, and consequences can be anticipated or predicted. Decision-makers are assumed to be rational, unbiased, capable of processing complete information, and able to anticipate consequences while identifying all possible alternatives. The desired outcome is to make a decision that maximizes the sought-after results.

Decisions under the classical model follow a series of five steps. First, the problem is formulated or identified, with the full and complete nature of the problem understood. Second, all alternative or potential solutions are listed. Third, all relevant data and information are gathered to find and evaluate the alternatives. Fourth, the best alternative is decided upon and implemented. Finally, the decision is evaluated to determine its impact according to predetermined outcomes. This evaluation process provides feedback on how closely the actual results align with the intended results. While the classical model provides a logical framework, its chief problem is that life rarely presents perfect situations.

In practice, decision-makers, administrators, and managers do not face clearly-defined problems or have all the information necessary, making their every decision fraught with risks and uncertainty. These challenges highlight the failures of classical theory assumptions and the unlikelihood of their achieving truly optimal decisions. Given these issues, the behavioral school of thought developed, with theories that recognized the cognitive limitations in people as decision-makers.

The administrative model of decision-making, also known as the behavioralist approach, is based on Herbert Simon's work as presented in *Administrative Behavior* (Simon, 1997). Simon defines administration as "getting things done" and introduces the concept of bounded rationality. This model recognizes that decision-makers operate with both internal and external constraints, which often lead to decisions that are less than optimal. Simon refers to this as satisficing— reaching a decision that is not perfect but good enough under the circumstances. In this model, alternatives are evaluated sequentially as they are identified, and the first satisfactory or sufficient solution is chosen.

Bounded rationality responds to the economic utility function theory, which suggests that people look for a wide range of choices and select the one that maximizes their utility. However, this theory is flawed because intentions and preferences change, and decision-makers never have all the relevant information or full knowledge of all of the consequences. Bounded rationality warns economists against predicting human behavior by using abstract models to identify what is rational.

Charles Lindblom offers another decision-making model with his concept of incrementalism, as described in his article "The Art of Muddling Through" (Shafritz, 2004, pp. 177–187). Lindblom explains how decisions are often made incrementally rather than all at once. Large or sudden changes often result in conflict and opposition, while incrementalism favors creating change gradually over time. Incremental decision-making allows stakeholders time to adjust to changes rather than having it thrust on them all at once.

Retrospective decision-making, as described by Nutt (1993), involves the effect decision-makers' biases have on the choice of alternatives. In this model, decision makers start out with a preferred solution in mind and focus on justifying that choice rather than considering other alternatives seriously. While the decision-maker believes they have logically arrived at the best decision, that decision is likely suboptimal and may not even satisfice under the circumstances.

WHAT EXTERNAL AND INTERNAL FORCES ACT ON DECISION-MAKING?

Decisions are not made in a vacuum or a lab where all variables are controlled. They are made in the real world by real people. The table below outlines examples of factors that influence decision-making in government.

Table 3.1: Factors that Influence Decision-Making in Government

External Factors	Internal Factors
Public opinion	Organizational culture
Media (news and social)	Costs and resources
Lobbying	Legal matters
Global pressures	Practicality
Industry	Opposing views/ideas from within
Economic conditions	Dogma
Timing	Political party pressures
Evidence availability	Previous commitments
Think Tanks	Intergovernmental matters
Social and demographic changes	Values

The lists provided are not exhaustive but serve to illustrate the vast sources of influence influencing governmental decision-making. Decision-making is complex enough on its own, and the challenges escalate exponentially when one considers the environment in which government officials make decisions.

Decision-makers are not perfectly rational actors; they bring their own biases and preferences to the process. Personal values, their upbringing, where they went to college and what they studied there, religious beliefs, age, gender, and past experiences all influence how individuals behave, think, and make decisions. All these variables ultimately influence their decisions. Additionally, the organizational environment affects decisions. Organizations adopt statements of values, vision statements, and mission statements, which they expect their management and staff to internalize and prioritize as important values and goals.

Technology also affects decision-making. Advances in technology connect people worldwide, making quick reactions possible. The 24/7 media cycle and social media allow people to disseminate information as events unfold, thus driving public opinion and, in turn, influencing governmental decision-makers. The days of smoke-filled back rooms are long over. Much of today's governance occurs in full public view. Decision-makers and public officials are acutely aware of this transparency and of their being watched.

ADMINISTRATIVE CONTROLS: TYPES AND STRATEGIES

How can public organizations protect against administrators diverting from the agency's primary goals and objectives? This brings us to the concept of control. Consider this example: when people get up in the morning, they generally don't worry about getting to work. Why? This is because their getting to work is facilitated by the controls in place between where they live and where they work. Roads are paved and maintained by public works; traffic lights and signs at intersections control traffic flow; lines painted on the road order traffic; speed limits and laws—like those banning cell phone use while driving—govern behavior. These controls promote safety, allowing people to focus on getting to work. Are these controls 100 percent effective? No. Accidents happen, and drivers can decide to go somewhere else or not even leave their house in the morning. Nevertheless, the roadway system supports their intention of getting to work efficiently.

Similarly, organizations design and implement controls to help achieve their primary goals—different types of controls usually referred to as internal controls. Frameworks for internal control, published by such organizations as the Committee of Sponsoring Organizations (COSO, 2019) and the International Standards Organizations (ISO, 2019), provide organizations with detailed guidelines for constructing their own system of controls. A new level of control, enterprise risk management (ERM), integrates internal controls with organizational strategic planning (COSO, 2019). Linking the two together protects mission alignment and facilitates goal and objective accomplishment.

Controls can be classified by their function. Preventive controls are designed to stop issues before they occur. Detective controls alert management when something goes wrong, and corrective controls allow management to fix those issues. In computerized systems, general controls protect hardware and software from unauthorized access, while application controls protect specific software applications. These include role-based access restrictions, login credentials, and input and output protections to keep data from being corrupted, deleted, viewed, or transmitted without proper authorization.

Beyond technical control measures, administrative controls take on significant functions in organizations, including supervision. Vetting, hiring, and training employees for specific jobs, as well as notice of periodic evaluations, are all examples of administrative controls that ensure standards are being met or exceeded. Workplace safety rules protect individuals from harm and organizations from losses due to accidents. Conflict-of-interest policies and ethics statements set behavioral standards. Employees often receive training and sign statements that disclose any conflicts or that acknowledge their having received and read these standards, ensuring accountability and alignment with organizational goals.

Controls in public administration come in many forms. Some tell us what we can't do; others tell us what we can do. Some controls allow for discretion; others leave none. Controls can focus on internal activities; others, on external activities. In the public sector, a significant issue arises with agency "capture," where regulatory agencies become influenced through various means by the businesses they oversee. This can occur when staff from the regulatory agency and the regulated businesses change employment, shifting from regulated to regulator and back again and creating conflicts of interest.

Another potential threat is the "iron triangle," described by Shafritz (2004) as a mutually supportive relationship between a congressional committee or subcommittee, a private interest group, and a related government agency (p. 80). Essentially, it's a relationship in which one hand washes the other. These relationships often operate not in the public's best interests but in the service of special interests, usually those that wield money and power. Collusion among conspirators within these triangles makes this difficult to uncover. This powerful collusion between participants makes the iron triangle hard to defeat—even if everyone knows it exists.

One fundamental truth about controls—regardless of their type or nature— is that if they are bypassed or overridden, they become ineffective. To protect against breakdowns, monitors are essential. At the federal level, auditors serve as these monitors, including internal auditors within inspector general offices and external auditors from the Government Accountability Office (GAO, 2019). State and local governments often have similar monitors, such as state auditors. Each state agency likely has a system of inspector generals while state legislatures likely have joint oversight committees that work closely with state auditors. Larger local governments may employ internal audit or inspector general functions. The smaller the local government, the less likely they are to have dedicated monitoring resources. Some local governments therefore employ audit committees that work with internal and external auditors to review audit results and ensure the government responds appropriately to any audit findings.

Another type of control that some governments employ is a "hotline" that employees may call to report waste, fraud, and abuse. The Freedom of Information Act (FOIA, 2019) is a control providing access to many government records in order to prevent officials from covering up actions against the public's best interests. A last resort control involves whistleblower protections shielding those who expose misconduct from retaliation. This part of unit six presents a general overview of public sector controls in place that are committed to protecting those the government serves. While most public administrators are honest and act with integrity, controls are necessary to protect against unintentional as well as intentional behavior contrary to the public good.

PERFORMANCE MEASUREMENT AND DETERMINING IMPACTS

To this point, we have examined decision-making and administrative controls. Now, we turn to the role of performance measurement in the public sector. Any properly designed system will include a monitoring and feedback loop. The decision-making process is incomplete without considering the actual effect of a decision against its intended effect. It is important to ask whether the decision was effective or not. For any decision, be it a policy or administrative one, it is important to assess whether and whether the desired results were achieved.

Performance measurement is a core element of New Public Management (NPM) (Osborne & Gaebler, 1992). As NPM grew in popularity, so did the focus on measuring the performance of government programs and activities. In 1993, the federal government institutionalized performance measurement with the Government Performance and Results Act (GPRA). The Act required government agencies covered under its provisions to adopt performance measurement practices. The goal was to help Congress assess the performance of government programs and activities and improve their effectiveness (Kettl, 1996). In 2010, the GPRA Modernization Act (GPRAMA) was enacted to update the tools for performance measurement and reporting, improving the information available to policymakers assessing effectiveness (GAO, 2011).

The emphasis on performance measurement also affected state and local governments. In 2010, the Government Finance Officers Association published *A Performance Management Framework for State and Local Government: From Measurement and Reporting to Management and Improving*. This report provided a recommended framework for state and local governments to consider in developing their own performance measurement systems (The National Performance Management Advisory Commission, 2010).

At the state level, Florida enacted the Performance and Accountability Act of 1994 (OPPAGA, 2019), which created the Office of Program Policy Analysis (OPPAGA) and enhanced the performance-auditing duties of the state's Auditor General. The Act required state agencies to develop, track, and report on key performance measures tied to the budgeting process. In Georgia, the Governor's Office of Planning and Budget maintains a website (Budget, 2019) for state agency strategic planning and performance measurement.

At the local level, cities are also adopting performance measurement and reporting practices. For example, the City of Augusta, Georgia, publishes a performance dashboard on its website (Augusta, 2019), allowing citizens to track the city's performance in various areas.

According to Hatry (2006), all agencies providing services to the public should be able to apply the principles of performance measurement (pp. 7–8). Most programs and activities performed by these agencies can be measured; the key lies in identifying what information should be measured. Hatry's *Performance Measurement: Getting Results* (2006) provides a well-laid-out explanation of how performance measurement works and how to implement it. Agencies need to identify what should be tracked, such as timeliness, accessibility, accuracy, satisfaction, quality, condition, and safety. The types of information tracked may include resource inputs, service outputs, program outcomes (both intermediate and final), key performance indicators (KPIs), and efficiency ratios. This information can then be organized and presented in various formats, such as written reports or performance dashboards. Some dashboards may be public-facing, while others may be for internal management use.

The key to performance measurement is defining impact. In some cases, policies are written so that impact is readily apparent or clearly defined, while in others, defining impact is more difficult. Nevertheless, impacts should be measurable. For example, the services of a Driver's License Office can be quite easily broken down into measurable outcomes. However, programs like services offered by a public affairs office may prove more challenging. For example, programs like a suicide prevention hotline may find it more difficult to define outcomes that clearly establish their impact. A common issue in performance measurement is establishing causality between an agency's activities and the resulting outcomes. The validity and legitimacy of performance measures will often depend on whether those viewing the results accept the link between the agency's activities and the reported results.

It is important to remember that people want to know what has been done for them lately. They want to know how their tax dollars are spent and whether those funds are used efficiently. Are the services provided effective? Is the government economical in its use of resources? These questions are unlikely to go away. Given today's focus on transparency and accountability, decisions will always be scrutinized to determine whether they were right and achieved their intended results. Public administrators must keep this in mind when implementing new policies, revising existing ones, or just serving the public in their daily jobs.

CONCLUSION

An essential part of every public administrator's job is decision-making. In this unit, we summarized the popular decision-making models: the classical model with its many assumptions, the administrative model, which focuses on the limits of human behavior, and the retrospective model, which focuses on the inherent biases in decision-making. Incrementalism was also discussed, a model that introduces gradual change over time rather than all at once. Decision-making is a complex task influenced by many factors, including characteristics of the individual, the organization, and external forces such as news media, social media, and popular opinion. Decisions are further constrained by the administrative controls existing within governments that are part of the legal framework impacting all the work of public administrators. Lastly, this unit addressed the role that performance management plays in decision-making. All decisions should be evaluated after implementation to determine whether the desired results were achieved and whether any adjustments are necessary.

Looking ahead to the 21ˢᵗ century, decision-making will increasingly be impacted by Big Data. Huge databases are being compiled, housing data on almost all aspects of life. The Government Performance and Results Act was amended in 2010 by the GPRA Modernization Act, which, according to the GAO, focuses on the use of data to make decisions and evaluate performance. The use of data is seen as a way to hold individuals and organizations accountable for achieving results. Data-driven decisions and post-implementation evaluation offer a rigorous and quantitative method for validating results, surpassing less quantitative methods. As a result, public administrators must know how to identify, collect, store, analyze, and use data to make informed decisions and evaluate their results effectively.

REFERENCES

Appleby, P. H. (1949). *Big democracy* (2nd ed.) New York, NY: Alfred A. Knopf.

City of Augusta. (2019). *Augusta performance dashboard.* Retrieved October 29, 2019, from https://augustaga.gov/1653/Performance-Dashboard

Committee of Sponsoring Organizations of the Treadway Commossion (COSO). 2019. Retrived October 29, 2019, from www.coso.org

Freedom of Information Act. (2019). Retrieved October 29, 2019, from www.foia.gov

Governor's Office of Planning and Budget. (2019). *Strategic planning.* Retrieved October 29, 2019, from https://opb.georgia.gov/planning-and-evaluation/strategic-planning

Hatry, H. P. (2006). *Performance measurement: Getting results.* Washington, D.C.: The Urban Institute Press.

International Organization for Standardization. (2019). Retrieved October 29, 2019, from www.iso.org

Kettl, D. (1996, March 6). Testimony: Implementation of the Government Performance and Results Act of 1993. Brookings Institution. Retrieved October 29, 2019, from https://www.brookings.edu/testimonies/implementation-of-the-government-performance-and-results-act-of-1993/

Nutt, P. C. (1993). The formulation processes and tactics used in organizational decision-making. *Organization Science*, 4(2), 226–51. www.jstor.org/stable/2635201

Office of Program Policy Analysis and Government Accountability. (2019). Retrieved October 29, 2019, from http://www.oppaga.state.fl.us/shell.aspx?pagepath=pb2.htm

Osborne, D., & Gaebler, T. (1992). *Reinventing government: How the entrepreneurial spirit is transforming the public sector from schoolhouse to statehouse, city hall to the Pentagon*. Reading, MA: Addison-Wesley.

Shafritz, J. M. (2004). *The dictionary of public policy and administration*. Boulder, CO: Westview Press.

Shafritz, J. M., & Hyde, A. C. (2004). *Classics of public administration*. Australia: Wadsworth/Cengage Learning.

Simon, H. (1997). *Administrative behavior: A study of decision-making processes in administrative organizations*. New York, NY: The Free Press.

The National Performance Management Advisory Commission. (2010). "Research reports." *Government Finance Officers Association*. Retrieved October 29, 2019, from https://www.gfoa.org/pm-commission-framework

U.S. Government Accountability Office. (2011). "Government performance: GPRA Modernization Act provides opportunities to help address fiscal, performance, and management challenges." Retrieved October 2019, from https://www.gao.gov/products/GAO-11-466T

—. (2019). Retrieved October 29, 2019, from www.gao.gov

—. (2020). Data-driven decision-making. Retrieved April 25, 2020, from www.gao.gov/key_issues/data-driven_decision_making/issue_summary

Public Policy

LEARNING OBJECTIVES

Students studying this unit should be able to:

1. Define the term public policy.
2. Briefly identify and explain the public policy theories.
3. List who decides on public policy.
4. Describe the public policy development process.
5. Summarize the challenges to implementing public policy.

INTRODUCTION

Whenever someone takes a road trip, it is important to know where they are going and how they plan to get there. One might use Google Maps to plan the trip and track it through a cell phone or the car's navigational system. The same is true for those using planes or boats, where flight or navigational plans are prepared and filed to document one's travel route. Businesses need to know where they are going as well. Private businesses focus on sales, profits, and costs to achieve desired profit levels. Nonprofit organizations focus on their mission, such as ending hunger, finding a cure for a disease, or raising funds or college scholarships. All the decisions these organizations make are designed to help them get where they want to go.

The same principle applies to the public sector. Governments need a way to communicate a course or direction, and that is the role of public policy. Thomas Dye (1972) defined public policy as "anything a government chooses to do or not to do" (p. 2). Shafritz (2004) describes it as "a policy made on behalf of a public by means of a public law or regulation that is put into effect by public administration." The term "public" refers to the scope of the policy, as it may affect many citizens. "Policy" refers to the course or direction being set. Shafritz states that a policy is "standing decision by an authoritative source such as a government, a corporation, or the head of a family" (Shafritz, 2004, p. 243).

Private businesses and nonprofits follow policies set by management. The senior levels of management set strategic policies, while middle and lower levels establish operational policies. All policies are designed to work in harmony with the mission or primary goal of the business. These entities typically adopt vision statements, mission statements, and statements of values that guide their behavior. They develop annual strategic plans mapping out how they intend to achieve their mission. These plans are then broken down into goals and objectives, applicable to all levels of the organization. Good strategic plans facilitate measuring the objectives to determine performance.

Governments also engage in strategic planning. Agencies often have mission statements and statements of values, along with goals and objectives. They generally produce reports or digital dashboards to demonstrate performance toward goal achievement. However, this activity is distinct from the public policy process. Businesses, nonprofits, and private citizens are all stakeholders in the public policy process, which is more political than a typical strategic planning process. As a result, it often leads to conflict.

Public policy communicates how governments intend to respond to issues, challenges, and problems. Immigration is an example of a current hot topic. Immigration policy is particularly complex because it impacts other policy areas, such as national security. When a policy is not clearly stated, those tasked with implementing it will struggle to carry out their responsibilities. Unclear policy creates confusion throughout the system, leaving government officials uncertain about how to respond to the situations they face. Therefore, policy must clearly express intent. Confusing or poorly articulated policies often lead to poor execution and mistakes.

PUBLIC POLICY THEORIES

To better understand public policy, it is helpful to use theoretical models. While we will spend only a brief amount of time covering these theories, it is important for students to recognize their existence and how they are used to explain policy decisions. Academics have identified many models that are helpful in explaining various aspects of public policy. Dye (1972) summarizes some of these models in his text *Understanding Public Policy*, presented here with very brief descriptions.

Table 5.1: Public Policy Models

Policy Model	Description
Institutional Model	Emphasizes the formal and legal aspects of government
Process Model	Focus on political systems theory and political responses to demands
Rational Model	Based on public choice and the motivations of individual actors
Incremental Model	Builds on past decisions, viewed as a slow and steady progression
Group Model	Pluralism; involves diverse and competing interests

Policy Model	Description
Elite Model	Wealthy and powerful interests influence values and preferences
Public Choice Model	Everyone involved acts based on their self-interests
Game Theory Model	Statistical approach to studying behavior and decision-making

No single theory explains all public policy decisions. Instead, multiple approaches are used to gain a deeper understanding. We will examine a few of these models in more detail by considering climate change policy.

Using institutionalism, we would focus on the role of different governments, treaties between governments, and regulatory frameworks within individual nations when evaluating appropriate policy options for climate change. With rational choice, the focus shifts to analyzing the costs and benefits of different policy options. Elite theory examines the influence of powerful groups seeking to shape policy outcomes, which may include political support measured through campaign contributions. Group models emphasize the competition between different interest groups and their impact on the policy process, such as environmental groups versus industry groups and their preferences for climate policy options.

Each model provides a distinct perspective on policy issues, highlighting different characteristics and aspects of the decision-making process.

WHO MAKES POLICY?

As noted earlier, many stakeholders are involved in the policy process. Each person or group brings their agenda to the table, aiming to be heard, influence outcomes, and protect their interests. Their involvement begins with identifying an issue or problem of concern. Once identified, the individual or group plans carefully and executes a campaign to place the issue on the legislature's agenda. Other individuals or groups, with differing agendas and priorities, may oppose the effort.

Stakeholders can include interest groups, professional organizations, lobbyists, and individual citizens, all of whom may attempt to initiate a legislative proposal. In the U.S. Congress, any member of the House of Representatives or the Senate has the authority to propose new legislation. Additionally, anyone can bring an issue before a legislative body by contacting their elected representatives, whether in person, through letters, email, or social media. The more supporters an issue has, the louder its voice. However, loud voices are not always enough.

The reality is that money often speaks louder. Those with financial resources typically have greater access to policymakers. Money flows from individuals, groups, and organizations to campaigns and parties, influencing the political process. As a result, the role of money and campaign financing has become an important and frequently debated topic in public policy.

Once an issue is placed on the agenda, it follows the legal legislative process as outlined by law, the Constitution, or, at the local level, a government charter. Legislators research, discuss, and debate bills, usually through a committee process at federal and state levels. If a bill survives committee review, it proceeds to the full legislative body for further debate and a vote. If passed, the bill is sent to the president or the equivalent executive officer at the state or local level for signature—or potentially a veto. A veto allows the executive to block legislation but is not available to all executive leaders.

The policy process is challenging to navigate. Most issues brought to the legislature never progress to the stage of becoming a bill, and many bills never make it into law.

EXECUTIVE POLICY PRIORITIES

Public policy often begins with a statement of preferences or a list of priorities. Presidents and governors often include their policy priorities on their official websites. While additional priorities may emerge during an executive's term in response to unfolding events, their performance is often evaluated based on their success in achieving the priorities initially outlined. Most priorities are broad enough to encompass various legislative and executive actions. We reviewed the websites of the Biden White House and the Georgia Governor's Office to identify the specific priorities of the president and the governor.

President Biden's site lists seven priorities.[1] When President Biden took office, the nation was still grappling with the effects of the COVID-19 pandemic, making pandemic response a key priority. A second priority focuses on addressing climate change, which includes modernizing infrastructure and transitioning to cleaner energy sources. The third priority is racial equity, acknowledging that biases and racial issues persist in the 21st century. Economic concerns make up the fourth priority, as the economy significantly influences elections and public sentiment: as the economy goes, so go many elections. Health care, the fifth priority, addresses rising costs and concerns over accessibility for all Americans. Immigration, the sixth priority, has garnered significant attention and coverage, particularly regarding illegal immigration and border security. The seventh and final priority is restoring America's global standing.

The website of the Governor of Georgia lists four main priorities: (1) making Georgia the top state for small businesses, (2) reforming state government, (3) strengthening rural Georgia, and (4) putting Georgians first. Each of these priorities is further broken into sub-priorities for implementing these main initiatives.[2] For example, to make Georgia more attractive to small businesses, the governor's initiatives include eliminating excessive rules and regulations, creating a competitive tax structure, ensuring a skilled workforce, modernizing logistics infrastructure, and improving online access to government information.

These priorities often originate during the chief executive's election campaign and are institutionalized into the administration once the candidate takes office.

---

1   White House Priorities.

2   Georgia Governor Priorities.

They are then integrated into the priorities of individual agencies headed by the chief executive's appointees. These priorities guide the development or revision of rules and regulations at the department and agency level and inform proposals for new legislation.

HOW IS POLICY DEVELOPED?

The policy-making process involves several steps or stages (Howlett & Ramesh, 2003). First, a problem or issue is placed on the legislature's agenda. Legislators and staff then work to develop the policy in the form of a bill. The bill undergoes a vetting process and, if successful, it is voted on by legislators from both houses. If the bill passes both houses, it is sent to the president (or governor at the state level) for approval. The president may either sign the bill into law or exercise veto power. If signed, the bill becomes law, and government agencies implement it by creating or modifying new regulations. Over time, the policy is evaluated, and revisions may occur during either the implementation or evaluation stages.

Public policies are often classified into four types, as described by T. J. Lowi (1964, 1972):

1. Distributive policies: Provide benefits to a few and allocate small costs to many.

2. Redistributive policies: Provide costly benefits to some and allocate those costs to others.

3. Regulatory policies: Control behavior of some kind and may levy penalties.

4. Constituent policies: Related to internal operations and civil servants within government agencies.

Public policy decisions are made at all levels of government—federal, state, and local—and the processes used to formulate and adopt policies are similar across all these levels. Public policies affect nearly every area of life. Lists of current policy issues can be found from various sources, such as the PEW Research Center, which periodically publishes articles listing public policy issues that Americans identify as important in polls (Bialik, 2019).

The table below presents a list of common public policy subjects along with examples of specific topics addressed in policy legislation, based on the author's general online research.

Table 5.2: Common Public Policy Subjects

Public Policy Subjects	Specific Policy Examples
Criminal Justice	Death penalty, drug policy, gun control
Culture and Society	Abortion, arts, civil rights, immigration
Economic Affairs	Budget, taxes

Public Policy Subjects	**Specific Policy Examples**
Education	Elementary, secondary, higher education
Environment	Air and water quality, climate change
Government Operations	Campaign finance, privatization
Health	Health care access, insurance, Medicare
Social Welfare	Social Security, WIC, Medicaid
Foreign Affairs	Aid
National Security	Military spending, Patriot Act
Agriculture	Support payments
Energy	Solar, wind, nuclear, fossil fuels

Examples of policy issues currently occupying state legislative agendas include federal deregulation, cybersecurity, privacy rights, marijuana use, state education systems, state taxes, budgeting and government spending, health care, and land development and use.

At the local level, legislative agendas often focus on issues such as property tax rates, local option sales tax (LOST) proposals and allocations, public safety (police, fire, and ambulance services), basic and enhanced community services, waste management, and education.

The Government Accountability Office (GAO) provides an informative website on the federal rulemaking process.[3] They break it down into three phases: (1) initiating action, (2) developing proposed action, and (3) developing final action. Each phase includes detailed steps. The first phase involves identifying the need for rules and gathering the necessary information to begin the process. The second phase focuses on drafting the proposed rules and publishing them for public review. The last phase starts with public vetting of the proposed rule,[4] followed by an editing process, and ends with the publication of the final rule.

Although some criticize the volume of rules and regulations, arguing that they function like laws without going through the formal legislative process, rules do provide structure and organization to policy implementation. As previously noted, laws result from the legislative process at either the federal or state level. Rulemaking, however, occurs within executive and independent agencies and is often less transparent.

The key takeaway is that public policy can address virtually any area of life. Legislative bodies across the country face an endless stream of issues and problems competing for attention. The policymaking process is designed to help them manage continuous influx.

To summarize, incoming elected officials typically outline their agendas as a set of policy priorities. These priorities are often pursued through legislative proposals, some of which become laws. Once a law is passed by the legislative body and signed

---

3 GAO Federal Rule Making.

4 Regulations.gov.

by the executive, the relevant agencies develop the regulations and rules needed for its implementation. This is a complex, time-consuming process that can take years to complete. Moreover, the process is cyclical, involving evaluation of the outcomes and revisions to the original policy.

WHAT ARE THE CHALLENGES IN IMPLEMENTING POLICY?

The process of getting a bill through the legislature and executive is challenging enough, but the difficulties do not end once a policy is enacted into law. The implementation process can be equally, if not more, complex. For example, in 2011, the State of Alabama enacted a law to address illegal immigration. At the time, it was considered the toughest immigration law in the United States. The law authorized police to detain suspected illegal immigrants based on visual identification and required employers to verify the legal status of all workers through an electronic verification system.

However, the new law led to unintended consequences in other areas that were neither anticipated nor necessarily intended during its passage. While addressing immigration issues, the law inadvertently caused a labor shortage, which had significant impacts on farming and the food supply. This raises the question: which problem is more critical?

The challenges in implementing public policy are numerous, often stemming from the nature of the problems themselves. Many problems are "wicked" problems—issues that are extremely difficult or even impossible to solve because attempts to address them often trigger other problems (Rittel & Webber, 1973). While not exhaustive, the following are some of the challenges faced in implementing public policies (Ahmed & Dantata, 2016).

Table 5.3: Challenges in Public Policy Implementation

Examples of Challenges in Public Policy Implementation
Complexity of the policy
Clarity of the law enacting the policy
Extent of political support and opposition to the policy
Impact of technology
Resources (funding, staffing, infrastructure)
Time (drafting and adopting regulations)
Enforcement issues

CONCLUSION

Public policy is about setting a course or direction for government. Policies provide the framework for administrators with their implementation and execution. Legislators define this direction by passing laws, while executive and independent agencies and departments implement those laws by adopting regulations and carrying out enforcement activities.

The process is not strictly black and white; instead, it more closely resembles a marble cake, with overlapping roles and responsibilities. Legislators often involve themselves in implementation, while administrations engage in policymaking. For example, the president of the United States influences and sometimes directly sets policy through their actions. Preparing the annual budget proposal for Congress is a policymaking act, and presidents frequently use executive orders to enact policy without going through Congress. Policy can also be created through statements to the media.

Legislators shape policy implementation by constraining options within the legislation itself. They may also exert political influence to informally guide how a policy is carried out or use their staff connections to communicate preferences regarding implementation.

Any discussion of public administration or public policy must take into account the interplay between the two. Isolating either activity oversimplifies the behavior of government.

REFERENCES

Bednar, V. (2013, April 29). *Making public policy more fun* [Video]. TEDxToronto. YouTube. https://youtu.be/wXYSsA5yVSY?si=n6kR4ibZUirHw1Mh

Dye, T. (1972). *Understanding public policy*. Englewood Cliffs, NJ: Prentice Hall.

FrontLine. (2015, October 20). *Immigration battle* [Documentary]. PBS. https://www.pbs.org/wgbh/frontline/film/immigration-battle/

Gregory, J. (2015, October 3). *Local option sales tax: Pros and cons*. KET Public Affairs. https://www.ket.org/public-affairs/local-option-sales-tax/

History Channel. (2019, May 14). *U.S. immigration timeline*. https://www.history.com/topics/immigration/immigration-united-states-timeline

Lowi, T. J. (1964). American business, public policy, case studies, and political theory. *World Politics, 16*(4), 177–181.

Lowi, T. J. (1972). Four systems of policy, politics, and choice. *Public Administration Review, 32*(4), 298–310.

Shafritz, J. (2004). *The dictionary of public policy and administration*. Boulder, CO: Westview Press.

Solman, P. (2011, October 28). *For undocumented workers, it's not-so-sweet home Alabama* [Video]. *PBS NewsHour*. PBS. https://www.pbs.org/newshour/show/farmers-workers-cope-with-impact-of-ala-immigration-law

Weaver, K. (2016, October 13). *Challenges in policy implementation part 1* [Video]. Stanford CDDRL. YouTube. https://youtu.be/Y8jYNq4AqdI?si=AvXEkWz19JCwa9Rw/

Weaver, K. (2016, October 13). *Challenges of policy implementation part 2* [Video]. Stanford CDDRL. YouTube. https://youtu.be/vsCnJpg4-yc?si=u4imMi_3Nt_Ddyet

LINKS REFERENCED

White House Priorities website: https://www.whitehouse.gov/priorities

Georgia Governor Priorities website: https://gov.georgia.gov/about-us/initiatives-and-priorities

GAO Federal Rule Making Website: https://www.gao.gov/federal-rulemaking#:~:text=The%20process%20for%20creating%20federal,and%20opportunities%20for%20public%20comments

Regulations.gov: https://www.regulations.gov/learn

Human Capital in Public Administration

LEARNING OBJECTIVES

Students studying this chapter should be able to:

1. Define the term human capital.
2. Briefly summarize the history of public sector human resources in the United States.
3. Explain the challenges facing the U.S. government in staffing their offices.
4. Discuss the current state of public employment in the United States.
5. Reflect on the impact of innovation and technology on public-sector employment.

INTRODUCTION

In the previous chapters (particularly chapters four and five), we examined decision-making and public policy in the public sector. The legislative process often leads to the continuation, modification, or creation of government programs. Once authorized and funded, these programs require people to lead, manage, and administer them effectively to achieve their objectives. This chapter will explore the history, role, and importance of individuals employed in the public sector. Before delving deeper into this topic, it is important to define a specific term and explain its intended use.

We titled this chapter with the term "human capital" for a reason. However, we recognize that this term has its detractors, so we want to address its use upfront. According to Shafritz (2004), human capital is defined as "a concept that views employees as assets in the same sense as financial capital (p. 148). It presupposes that an investment in human potential will yield significant returns for the organization." Some critics argue that the term dehumanizes individuals and does not account for their intrinsic worth. However, it is difficult to argue against the idea that an organization's people are not its valuable assets.

For instance, take the Walt Disney Company. In its 2023 annual report (see references for the link), the company begins by addressing the importance its workforce to its success. On page two, part one, item one, Disney states that its "key human capital management objectives are to attract, retain, and develop the highest quality talent." The report further describes how human resource programs are designed to achieve these objectives.

Similarly, the Federal Office of Personnel Management (OPM) defines its mission as being "champions of talent for the federal government." OPM sees itself as a mechanism for positioning the federal government "as a model employer...through innovation, inclusivity, and leadership." Its vision is to "build a rewarding culture that empowers the workforce to solve some of the nation's toughest challenges."

The State of Georgia's Department of Administrative Services Human Resources Administration website expresses a similar view, stating that it creates "enterprise-wide HR programs that help agencies attract, develop, and retain a high-performing workforce." The neighboring state of Florida takes an even more direct approach. The website for the Department of Management Services Workforce Operations, State Human Resource Management, states, "Florida's state employees are our most valuable resource. They are the face of state government, and they provide the necessary service to address the needs of the State of Florida."

We will begin by briefly explaining the origins of the term and why it was coined. Following this, we will provide an overview of the history of human resource management in the United States. Next, we will summarize the current state of government employment in the United States. Toward the end of this chapter, we will discuss the challenges facing human resource management in the public sector and examine the impact of innovation and technology on public sector human resource management.

ORIGINS OF THE TERM HUMAN CAPITAL

When we discuss capital, we generally refer to assets owned and controlled by an individual or organization that are used to generate income and increase perceived value. These might include cash, investments, and physical items such as equipment, furniture, fixtures, buildings, and land. However, according to economists like Jacob Mincer (1958) and Gary Becker (n.d.), capital can also refer to people—or more precisely, the investment in training and education that individuals internalize. By investing in knowledge, skills, and abilities, individuals can increase their earning potential and improve their quality of life.

According to Eide and Showalter (2010), the concept of human capital—while not the term itself—was alluded to in Adam Smith's seminal work, *Wealth of Nations* (Smith & Griffith, 2012). Smith discussed the link between the wealth and prosperity of nations and the abilities of their people. Over the 20th century, an entire line of economic research developed, focusing on identifying, measuring, and explaining the value of education and training. It is now a well-established fact that graduating from high school and pursuing further education—whether in college or trade school—benefits not only the individual but also the community and society as a whole. Because of the importance of this topic, we provide an extensive list of resources for those interested in further reading and study.

While some may criticize the use of the term "human capital," we view it as a recognition of the central role people play in delivering government services, implementing policies and achieving their objectives, and meeting citizens' needs. Rather than dehumanizing the workforce, the term elevates their importance within the organization and acknowledges their inherent value to its success. With this belief and attitude, we undertake this introduction to the role of human capital in government across the United States.

HISTORY OF PUBLIC SECTOR HUMAN RESOURCES IN THE U.S.

The history of public employment in the United States is dynamic, reflecting changes in the nature of government employment in the United States from the nation's founding to the present day. As discussed in our earlier chapter on Constitutional foundations, the size of government has generally grown since 1789. This growth coincided with an increase in the size and complexity of the workforce and the evolving composition of the human capital needed to run the government's various units. This section provides a brief overview of the broad shifts in thinking about government employment from 1789 to the present.

Patricia Wallace Ingraham's *The Foundation of Merit* (1995) is an excellent source of information on the history of public service in the United States. Based on this work and others, we can identify three broad periods in the evolution of public employment: (1) the gentlemen's period, (2) the patronage/spoils period, and (3) the merit period.

The first period, the gentlemen's period, was characterized by those serving out of a sense of duty and honor. It was male-dominated and included individuals from the landed elite. Appointments during this time focused on character and competence.

The second period, the patronage or spoils system, focused on individuals' connections and ties. This period, which enjoyed its "hay" days from about 1830 to 1880, was marked by the use of government jobs as rewards for loyalty to a particular candidate or party. When a candidate was elected, their term began with replacing all existing employees with their own people. Qualifications for public service derived not from competence and character but from the willingness of those in positions of responsibility and authority of doing what the elected officials wanted them to do, in other words, of playing along with the power structure in place. This ultimately-inefficient system led to a rise in political corruption and general mistrust in the government—since it served a select few rather than the people in general.

The last and current period, the merit period, involved reform and the growth of a tiered employment system, with an increasing number of positions filled through a competitive recruitment process. This shift is generally thought to have begun with the passage of the Pendleton Act in 1883. This legislative reform aimed at professionalizing government service and protecting against the "evils" of the patronage or spoils system and has continued to evolve the civil service reform era into its present form. Since then, Congress has enacted reforms to improve employment with the federal government.

The following legislative measures, while not exhaustive, illustrate significant reforms that have shaped the modern civil service, addressing the inefficiencies and inequities of earlier systems and reinforcing the principles of merit-based public service.

In 1912, Congress took further steps to reform the civil service by passing the Lloyd-La Follette Act (U.S. Merit Systems Protection Board). This legislation protected certain civil service employees from being discharged for engaging in union activities or petitioning Congress. Some consider this the first in a line of whistleblower protection laws.

In 1920, Congress enacted the Civil Service Retirement Act, providing the first retirement benefits to civil service employees. These benefits were determined based on length of service and salary. Later, in 1939, the Hatch Act was passed (and subsequently amended multiple times). This law forbade federal employees from participating in certain partisan political activities or using their positions for partisan purposes (U.S. Congressional Research Service).

Nearly 40 years later, the Civil Service Reform Act of 1978 was signed into law. Through this legislation, Congress established the Office of Personnel Management (OPM) and the Merit Systems Protection Board (MSPB), among other reform initiatives, to further strengthen and protect the integrity, professionalism, and efficiency of public employment (U.S. Office of Personnel Management).

In 1989, Congress passed the Whistleblower Protection Act, addressing the need to protect individuals who speak out when they become aware of corruption, fraud, waste, and abuse within the government. This Act aimed to protect whistleblowers from retaliation and retribution by those impacted by their disclosures. It reinforced Congress's concern and focus on enhancing accountability and transparency in government. By fostering an environment where individuals could safely disclose misconduct, Congress sought to encourage, build, and sustain public trust in government. Nevertheless, various polls over the years indicate that public trust continues to be a concern.

In addition to trust, governments face many other challenges. These challenges, along with the government's response to them, will affect those in public service and those in human resource management. In the next section, we will explore some of these challenges.

CHALLENGES FACING PUBLIC SECTOR HUMAN RESOURCES

There are many challenges facing those responsible for managing the human resources function in the public sector. These challenges can be summarized into several categories: recruitment and retention, diversity and inclusion, technology, budget constraints, succession planning, bureaucracy, morale and engagement, and cybersecurity challenges. Government organizations at all levels must develop strategies and operating practices to address these challenges and seek benefits from the new technologies introduced into the public sector. In the next section, we will discuss some of these innovations and their possible benefits. For now, we will focus on the challenges they pose.

As the baby boomer generation ages and governments experience greater numbers of retirements, they will face challenges in finding replacements. The population in the United States is not growing significantly, which means the pool of potential candidates to replace those who retire is smaller, and governments face stiff competition from the private sector for their services. The shrinking pool of candidates also means that governments may have to contend with higher turnover rates as people are more mobile and may seek perceived better opportunities. Chief among the challenges facing HR in the public sector is navigating the bureaucracy.

Governments face a more rigid environment due to complex regulations and administrative practices, particularly in the recruitment, hiring, and retention of employees. The regulatory environment can be rigid, but it is also more political than most. This often leads to challenges in identifying and selecting the best candidates for a position when there may be pressure to select candidates based on affiliations and relationships. Another challenge facing workforce management in the public sector is the prevalence of unions and other collective or regulatory frameworks governing promotions and salary adjustments.

The lack of flexibility in workforce management became more particularly evident during the COVID-19 pandemic. The nationwide crisis resulted in a massive shift from working in centralized offices to working remotely from home. This shift was challenging for organizations accustomed to working from a centralized office where citizens could come for assistance and services. As restrictions loosened and organizations began reopening their offices, the country saw more people dropping out of the workforce or changing jobs to ones that were more accepting of the new remote work arrangements.

The shifting workplace pressures, the development of new technologies facilitating these shifts, and the shrinking workforce pool create a pressure-filled environment that makes it challenging for organizations with inflexible workforce management systems to succeed. Governments will need to cope with these challenges to find, hire, and retain new employees with the skills and abilities critical to operating a modern workplace environment or risk not being able to maintain a level of service acceptable to constituents. The risk is particularly high in an environment influenced by the political winds of change from election to election.

Given the challenges faced in managing the human capital necessary to deliver services to citizens at all levels of government, we next want to briefly examine the current state of public sector employment. Governments must respond to these challenges in meaningful ways or risk losing intellectual capital they cannot replace from those who have long served them, while struggling to find the next generation of public servants to take their place. There is a clear need to facilitate the transfer of knowledge and expertise from those leaving public service to those entering it.

CURRENT STATE OF PUBLIC SECTOR EMPLOYMENT IN THE U.S.

Based on economic data from the U.S. Bureau of Labor Statistics (FRED), as of 2024, there are nearly 24 million government employees across the United States, with nearly 3 million employed in the federal government. This represents significant growth since the 1940s when total government employment was approximately 4 million. Federal employment has remained stable since the end of World War II and the Korean War. However, while overall government employment has increased, trust in government has not. According to the PEW Foundation,[1] only 1% of Americans trust the federal government to do what is right "just about always," and only 15% believe the government will do what is right "most of the time." Other organizations, such as Gallup, have conducted similar surveys and reported comparable findings. This lack of trust in government likely impacts those currently working in government and may influence the decisions of individuals considering their first or next employment opportunity.

The size of the government workforce relative to the total workforce is roughly 15%, with about 2% classified as federal employees (based on a Google search). The exact numbers vary depending on the data source (BLS, Brookings, USAFacts, or NASRA). While these numbers may seem manageable in scope, they still represent a significant portion of the workforce. Coupled with an aging workforce nearing retirement, a looming challenge becomes apparent. According to the OPM Retirement webpage, 114,505 federal employees retired in a single year, and since 2000, there has been an upward trend in the number of annual retirements. Given these numbers, what steps is the government taking to manage the need to replace retirees and ensure continuity of services moving forward?

The GAO, on its website page covering human capital management, outlines several actions federal agencies should consider in addressing the challenge of filling vacant positions. First, agencies are encouraged to develop long-term strategies for recruiting, developing, and retaining talent. In developing their workforce, agencies should adopt strategic, data-driven approaches based on training and development, ensuring employees have the most current skills and abilities

---

1   https://www.pewresearch.org/topic/politics-policy/trust-in-government/

to succeed. Performance management systems should clearly communicate expectations and hold employees accountable for results. Additionally, GAO recommends placing greater emphasis on DEI (diversity, equity, and inclusion) efforts to ensure employees feel connected. Succession planning should focus on developing critical skills and offering stretch assignments to staff with potential for promotion.

The Office of Management and Budget (OMB) places significant emphasis on strategic human capital management (SHCM) in *Circular A-11, Preparation, Submission, and Execution of the Budget.* Agency Chief Human Capital Officers (CHCO) align human capital practices with agency goals and objectives. Human capital management is integral to an agency's annual strategic planning and budgeting process. The OPM, OMB, and individual agencies recognize the importance of a motivated and focused workforce in providing services that meet constituent expectations. Key areas highlighted by the OMB include performance evaluation, training and development, and wellness programs.

Managing human capital to support the government's strategic and operational goals is also a concern for state and local human resource management. Summarizing efforts at these levels is more challenging because, unlike the single federal government, there are fifty states and thousands of local governments. However, recent academic research and professional journalism have offered insights into these efforts. Several articles from *Governing Magazine* between 2017 and 2023 outline the challenges and responses of local government human capital management.

Howard (2017) described an environment in local governments recovering from the 2000s recession, marked by budget stress, reduced staffing levels, heightened expectations and performance, increased retirements, and tight labor markets. Governments struggled to recruit, hire, and retain qualified personnel challenging due to inflexible legacy systems and low pay scales. Howard recommended reviewing existing civil service rules and regulations, assessing current human resource practices, and adopting goal-based management practices. Howard also noted the growing trend of governments creating chief human resource officer roles to better manage these processes.

By 2022 (Smith, 2022), budgets were no longer the pressing issue they had been in earlier years, as governments had largely recovered from financial constraints. However, addressing human capital needs remained a slow process. Governments, like the private sector, faced the challenges of a post-pandemic recovery after COVID-19. They experienced higher quit rates post-pandemic but continued to face steady or increased service demands and constituent expectations for quality. Recruiting and retaining qualified personnel remained difficult requiring governments to adopt more innovative practices.

These practices included increasing HR system agility, utilizing social media, encouraging employee referrals, and offering sign-on bonuses. Governments also began implementing flexible work arrangements, including remote work, allowing them to "cast a wider net" geographically to attract employees. Additionally, governments started focusing on branding as a strategy to attract qualified applicants.

Lavigna (2023) summarized a half dozen strategies that governments could consider to help alleviate the challenges faced in human capital management. He recommended addressing pay problems to make government jobs more competitive in the employment marketplace. Among other actions, he noted that governments should eliminate nonessential hiring requirements, make more timely hiring decisions, and increase their focus on diversity, equity, and inclusion issues. These efforts would help build employee engagement, morale, and motivation. Finally, Lavigna suggested increasing the effective use of technology and data analytics to support important human capital decisions. Interestingly, this last recommendation appeared to contradict a point made by Smith (2022) in the earlier article, where Smith emphasized that leadership should spend more time listening to aid decision-making.

The information presented in the *Governing* articles aligns with the academic research we examined. Jacobson and Sowa (2016) presented the results of a 2012 survey of HR directors and municipal clerks in Colorado and North Carolina. The survey sought responses to two prompts: (1) What do you see as the biggest challenges facing municipal governments in terms of managing their workforces? (2) If possible, please share an HRM innovation that has improved how your municipality manages its people. The authors summarized these responses into three categories: First, limited resources and staff to meet needs, including funding, time, and headcount; second, maintaining and recruiting a motivated workforce, which involved finding, developing, and retaining talent, building morale, and addressing demographic issues; and third, a range of other issues, such as manager skill, legal mandates, political interference, and public perception. Unfortunately, few of the respondents indicated any innovations being undertaken.

Perlman (2016), in a related article, shared insights from interviews with three HR directors—two from county governments (Georgia and Michigan) and one from a municipal government (California). The directors mentioned resource limitations, recruitment and retention problems, morale and motivation issues, and the need for leadership development and succession planning.

More recently, and post-pandemic, Wesemann (2024) summarized findings from a survey of employees in the city of Tempe, Arizona. The research examined the relationship between strategic human capital management (SHCM), employee job satisfaction, and voluntary turnover intention. The survey results indicated that support from immediate supervisors, professional development opportunities, and employee engagement activities were the most critical factors within SHCM.

All the research points to the importance of people to their organizations. Employees are an invaluable resource, contributing through their knowledge, skills, and abilities (KSAs). The role of HR management—specifically strategic human capital management—is to provide an environment that promotes high levels of job satisfaction and achieves positive organizational outcomes. Motivated and engaged employees will lead to enhanced productivity and help reduce organizational costs.

IMPACT OF INNOVATION AND TECHNOLOGY ON PUBLIC SECTOR HUMAN RESOURCES

Innovation and technology are changing how human resource (HR) management is conducted. Advances in technology are fueling innovation in this field, as in others. These impacts cut across all areas of HR management, including recruitment and hiring, training and development, performance management, employment arrangements, and employee engagement and communication. The evolution of technology has enabled the increased use of data analytics and predictive modeling in HR, as well as the increase in remote and online options. There is no sign of a slowdown, as the spread of artificial intelligence promises to offer even greater opportunities for efficiency and effectiveness in HR management.

Technology has significantly impacted recruitment and hiring through increased access and automation. The Internet has moved the recruitment and application process online, utilizing job boards, posting services, and organizational websites to advertise positions and facilitate applications. With advances in technology, applicants can now upload resumes and allow systems to auto-populate applications using the information, speeding up the process. These systems also enable automated applicant tracking. Job fairs and interviews can now be conducted online, adding further convenience. Once hired, performance management is increasingly supported by technology. HR systems with intelligent performance management features streamline the evaluation process, simplifying tasks such as setting goals, tracking progress, and crafting feedback, including areas for improvement.

Technology has also led to innovations in work arrangements. Coupled with the impact of the COVID-19 pandemic, organizations are increasingly adopting remote work and using video conferencing for meetings. Employees are no longer required to work exclusively from a central or field office; they can now work from home while staying connected with colleagues and others to carry out their duties and responsibilities. Platforms like Teams, Zoom, and Webex offer tools ranging from basic video conferencing to advanced work team engagement features. Employees across cities, counties, states, or even countries can collaborate, coordinate, and manage projects the need for travel. This increases efficiency and reduces the business costs by minimizing travel expenses.

These technologies have similarly changed training and development. As training needs increase, organizations are shifting from in-person sessions at physical locations to online training that can be conducted synchronously or asynchronously, depending on organizational needs. With the rise in security risks, including hacking, ransomware attacks, and data theft, IT security training organizations required has expanded. Much of this training is now delivered virtually through prerecorded modules with controls to ensure participants watch, pay attention to, and complete the material.

Innovation will continue to shape the future of human resource management. Advances in data analytics and predictive modeling will make it possible for officials to make better-informed decisions regarding workforce planning, talent management, and resource allocation. New technology facilitates the analysis of larger amounts of data, including big data, so that officials can model future staffing needs and develop comprehensive strategies to address current and future workforce challenges.

CONCLUSION

It should be clear after studying this chapter that managing human capital is an important function and policy area within public administration. Regardless of the impact of technology, people will remain a critical resource for public organizations in delivering quality services to a demanding and often critical public. Managers in the public sector would be well advised to be knowledgeable about issues related to human resources management. Turnover, whether voluntary or involuntary, is costly to an organization. Voluntary turnover, in particular, results in the loss of significant institutional knowledge that is difficult to replace.

The employment market is competitive, and engaging in this marketplace requires a strategic approach that considers a lifecycle approach to recruiting, hiring, developing, and retaining an organization's most valuable resource. Government organizations must consider new ways of doing business when managing their human capital. Candidates now search for positions using social media platforms like Indeed and LinkedIn. Hiring decisions must be made promptly, and offers must be competitive. This likely requires changes to existing processes, rules, and regulations adopted long ago that impact hiring and onboarding. Attracting candidates also requires a fresh approach to marketing government jobs and their locations.

Once hired and onboarded, government organizations must invest in their workforce. This requires thoughtful, timely, and relevant training and development programs, often delivered using modern web-based technology. The health and well-being of employees must also be nurtured, as a healthy and happy workforce is likely to be more productive. Governments must have in place effective succession plans that demonstrate to candidates and new hires career paths, including opportunities leading to promotions and increased professional challenges, and competitive pay increases.

Managing human capital is and will remain an essential function in public sector organizations. Investing in people—an organization's human capital—is as important as investing in its physical capital.

REFERENCES

Becker, G. S. (n.d.). Human capital. In *The concise encyclopedia of economics*. Library of Economics and Liberty. Retrieved April 4, 2024, from https://www.econlib.org/library/Enc/HumanCapital.html

Department of Administrative Services, State of Georgia. (n.d.). *Human resources administration*. Retrieved March 15, 2024, from https://doas.ga.gov/human-resources-administration

Department of Management Services, State of Florida. (n.d.). *State human resource management*. Retrieved March 16, 2024, from https://www.dms.myflorida.com/workforce_operations/state_human_resource_management

Eide, E.R., and Showalter, M.H. (2010). Human capital. In P. Peterson, E. Baker, and B. McGaw (Eds.), *International encyclopedia of education* (3rd ed., pp. 282–287). Elsevier. https://doi.org/10.1016/B978-0-08-044894-7.01213-6

U. S. Government Accountability Office. (n.d.). *Human capital management*. Retrieved from https://www.gao.gov/human-capital-management

Ingraham, P. W. (1995). *The foundation of merit: Public service in American democracy*. Johns Hopkins University Press.

Jacobson, W. S., & Sowa, J. E. (2015). Strategic human capital management in municipal government: An assessment of implementation practices. *Public Personnel Management, 44*(3), 317–339. https://doi.org/10.1177/0091026015591283

Lavigna, R. J. (2023, March 2). A road map for dealing with government's workforce crisis. *Governing*. Retrieved April 10, 2024, from https://www.governing.com/work/a-road-map-for-dealing-with-governments-workforce-crisis

Mincer, J. (1958). Investment in human capital and personal income distribution. *Journal of Political Economy, 66*(4), 281–302. http://www.jstor.org/stable/1827422

Novak, W. K. (2020, April 20). *The Hatch Act: A primer* (CRS Report No. IF11512). Retrieved April 10, 2024, https://crsreports.congress.gov

Office of the Whistleblower Ombuds. (n.d.). *Resources*. Retrieved April 10, 2024, from https://whistleblower.house.gov/resources/whistleblower-audience

Perlman, B. J. (2016). Human resource management at the local level: Strategic thinking and tactical action. *State and Local Government Review, 48*(2), 114–120. https://www.jstor.org/stable/44651987

Pew Research Center. (n.d.) Trust in government. Retrieved April 5, 2024, from https://www.pewresearch.org/topic/politics-policy/trust-in-government/

Risher, H. (2017, May 19). HR's crucial role in boasting government's performance. *Governing*. Retrieved April 10, 2024, from https://www.governing.com/archive/col-human-resources-hr-crucial-role-boosting-government-performance.html

Shafritz, J. M. (2004). *The dictionary of public policy and administration*. Westview Press.

Smith, A., Spencer, M. G., & Griffith, T. (2012). *Wealth of nations*. Wordsworth Editions.

Smith, C. (2022). Local governments search for answers to hiring challenges. *Governing*. Retrieved April 10, 2024, from https://www.governing.com/work/local-governments-search-for-answers-to-hiring-challenges

U.S. Bureau of Labor Statistics. (n.d.). *All employees, federal* [CES9091000001]. FRED, Federal Reserve Bank of St. Louis. Retrieved April 5, 2024, from https://fred.stlouisfed.org/series/CES9091000001

U.S. Bureau of Labor Statistics. (n.d.). *All employees, government* [USGOVT]. FRED, Federal Reserve Bank of St. Louis. Retrieved April 5, 2024, from https://fred.stlouisfed.org/series/USGOVT

U.S. Merit Systems Protection Board. (n.d.). *Merit system principle 9: Whistleblower protection*. Retrieved April 10, 2024, from https://mspb.gov/msp/msp9.htm

U.S. Office of Personnel Management. (n.d.). *Mission & history*. Retrieved March 15, 2024, from https://www.opm.gov/about-us/mission-history/

U.S. Office of Personnel Management. (n.d.). *Retirement statistics*. Retrieved April 7, 2024, from https://www.opm.gov/retirement-center/retirement-statistics/

Walt Disney Company. (2023). *Fiscal year 2023 annual financial report*. Retrieved March 15, 2024, from https://thewaltdisneycompany.com/investor-relations/

Wesemann, A. (2024). Turbulence ahead: Strategic human capital management, job satisfaction, and turnover intention. *Public Personnel Management, 53*(1), 148–169. https://doi.org/10.1177/00910260231192482

7 Ethics in the Public Sector

LEARNING OBJECTIVES

Students studying this chapter should be able to:

1. Define ethics and explain its importance in public administration.
2. Explain how the ethical conduct of members of government is managed in the U.S.
3. Describe a relevant ethical decision-making model and its use.
4. Explain the ethical challenges present in the 21st century.

INTRODUCTION

In chapter one, we defined public administration, and in chapter two, we explained its constitutional foundations. In this chapter, we will explore the ethical foundations of public administration. The U.S. Constitution does not specifically address ethics; it focuses on the legal foundation of government. However, one could argue that the legal foundation established by the framers is based on an ethical or moral foundation (Richardson and Nigro, 1987). In a letter to the Massachusetts Militia dated October 11, 1798, John Adams wrote, "Our constitution was made only for a moral and religious people. It is wholly inadequate to the government of any other."

Further, an introduction to the annotated Constitution explains approaches to interpreting that document and includes moral or ethical reasoning as one such approach (Congressional Research Service, n.d.). The authors of the introduction discuss a school of thought that contends the Constitution is infused with moral principles, such as "equal protection" and "due process." They further note that the Supreme Court often relies on these moral or ethical principles in deciding cases, such as *Lawrence v. Texas*.

Additional evidence of our Constitution's ethical or moral foundation is found in the language of the Declaration of Independence. The argument for rebelling against British rule over the colonies included an ethical or moral argument. In the document's first paragraph, the writers refer to "the Laws of Nature and of Nature's God" when addressing the relative equality that should be recognized as existing among and between people. They further argue that certain "truths" are "self-evident" and certain rights are "unalienable" and "endowed by their Creator." Among those rights life, liberty, and the pursuit of happiness. The writers argue that governments derive their power from those governed and that citizens should expect their government to protect their rights or risk losing the support of those governed. Thus, the foundation upon which our Constitution was laid included a belief in an established set of moral or ethical principles, with trust and accountability as the product of a government's adherence to those principles.

Given the central role of accountability, trust, and morals in founding our government, it is critical that public administration students be introduced to the importance of ethics in government early in their studies. Although most entering public service will do so through traditional means, such as applying, interviewing, and being hired as a staff member in an agency or department, ethics will play a crucial role in the exercise of discretionary decision-making. While we are governed by laws, the laws are not black and white. They include much that is gray and require interpretation, which results in discretionary decisions. A firm ethical foundation is essential to ensuring that decisions are not made from self-interest or other corrupt motivations.

In this chapter, we will begin our study of ethics by examining some definitions of ethics and explaining their importance in public administration. Following the definitions, there will be a discussion of how ethics is managed at different levels of government in the United States. We will then provide students with a breakdown of ethical governance at the federal, state, and local levels of government. Given the professional and applied nature of public administration, it is important that students learn about ethical decision-making frameworks and how they are applied (Svara, 2014). Finally, the pace of technological change is phenomenal and is challenging these ethical laws and frameworks. We will briefly discuss the challenges that developments in technology, such as artificial intelligence, place on systems of ethical decision making.

DEFINITIONS OF ETHICS AND ITS IMPORTANCE IN PUBLIC ADMINISTRATION

According to the Encyclopedia Britannica, ethics is a branch of philosophy concerned with standards of behavior. While many people use the terms "morals" and "ethics" interchangeably, some argue there is a distinction. An article in the *Encyclopedia Britannica* states that some define morals as normative and individual (Grannan, 2023), whereas ethics is defined as communal standards (Singer, 2023). Paul Appleby (1952) used the term "morality" interchangeably with "ethics" in a series of lectures he delivered at Louisiana State University. For our purposes, we will not bother with the distinction and will use the terms ethics and morality interchangeably.

Shafritz (2004) defines ethics as "A set of moral principles or values that can be applied to societies or social groups as a whole but that may also involve standards of behavior constituting implied responsibilities for professional activity" (p. 106). This definition aligns with those found in most standard dictionaries. Merriam-Webster (n.d.) defines ethics as "a set of moral principles or principles of conduct governing an individual or a group." Other definitions of ethics mirror these basic ideas. Ethical standards of behavior provide the framework through which society operates effectively. Research has established this as a fact of organizational life. Adherence to ethical standards of behavior makes trust possible.

Many universities across the country have established centers of ethics that promote, support, and disseminate research on ethics and offer programs focused on applied ethics in various organizational settings. One such center is the Markkula Center for Applied Ethics at Santa Clara University. They define ethics generally as "well-founded standards of right and wrong that prescribe what humans out to do, usually in terms of rights, obligations, benefits to society, fairness or specific virtues." They further differentiate ethical standards from feelings, laws, and social norms. Government ethics is described in slightly different terms. Their website states that "when governments serve the public interest and avoid engaging in behavior that promotes private interest, they are acting for the common good."

Paul Appleby (1952) stated, "It is not merely bigger government that ultimately matters: what is significant is that morality in administration alone could ensure better government" (p. 13). He argued in his lectures that morality and administration cannot be separated. It is the job of those in government to serve the public interest and not their own. The sentiment expressed at the Markkula Center for Applied Ethics (n.d.) echoes this same idea. H. George Frederickson (1997) argued that the role of ethics in administration is to reduce corruption in government (pp. 157–158). While he contended that administration is concrete and ethics abstract, he noted that they inform one another, as evidenced by the presence of codes and structures aimed at mitigating corruption and conflicts of interest.

Ethics in government is significant enough to take center stage in the study of public administration (Cohen & Eimicke, 1995). The ethical behavior of our public servants, whether elected or appointed, has been of concern throughout the history of our nation. While this is not intended to be a comprehensive history of ethics reform in the United States, it is important to have a brief understanding of the evolution of ethics in government from our founding to the present. We will summarize the major periods of ethical climate our nation has experienced (Ingraham, 1995; Locke, 1995; Open AI, 2024[1]).

Since the nation's founding in the late 18th century, the Founding Fathers emphasized virtue and ethical behavior, grounded in democratic ideals and the

---

1   The information contained in the table was obtained with a prompt using OpenAI, ChatGPT 3.5. See reference list.

rule of law. They believed that power and the permission to govern were granted by the people and that certain values and morals were established by a higher power. However, as the nation grew, so too did temptations to act out of personal self-interest, leading to corruption infiltrating the system established by the founders.

As discussed in chapter six, the 19th century was marked by the development of the spoils system, built on a foundation of unethical behavior and corruption. During this period, emphasis shifted from virtue and ethics to personal interest and political loyalties. Public offices, government jobs, and public contracts were frequently bought and sold.

Concerns over the pervasiveness of corruption at all levels of government gave rise to the Progressive Era, spanning the late 19th to early 20th centuries. This period was characterized by an increased focus on mitigating corruption and emphasizing accountability in government. It led to the passage of numerous key laws addressing corruption, corporate power, and social injustices. Examples of major pieces of legislation are summarized in the following table.

Table 7.1: Major Legislation Passed During the Progressive Era

Legislation	Year	Purpose/Key Provisions
Pure Food and Drug Act	1906	Regulated the safety and labeling of food and drugs; a response to unsanitary conditions in the meatpacking industry.
Sherman Antitrust Act	1890	Aimed to prevent anticompetitive practices and monopolies.
Clayton Antitrust Act	1914	Strengthened antitrust laws, clarified, and expanded provisions against anticompetitive behavior.
Federal Reserve Act	1913	Established the Federal Reserve System to stabilize the banking system and regulate monetary policy.
16th Amendment	1913	Granted Congress the power to levy income taxes.
17th Amendment	1913	Provided for the direct election of U.S. Senators by the people.
Keating-Owen Act	1916	Prohibited the interstate sale of goods produced by underage workers; addressed child labor abuses.
Adamson Act	1916	Established an eight-hour workday for railroad workers and provided overtime pay.
Smith-Lever Act	1914	Created the Cooperative Extension Service to disseminate agricultural and home economics knowledge.

The Watergate scandal (1974) during the Nixon Presidency in the late 1960s and early 1970s brought further scrutiny to the ethical climate in government. The post-Watergate period led to significant government reforms, including the passage of the Ethics in Government Act of 1978. This act established the Office of Government Ethics (OGE) to oversee and enforce ethical standards and created the

Independent Office of Special Counsel (Strauss, 2023, May 30b). These measures aimed to address unethical behavior and conflicts of interest by public officials.

Concerns about the influence of lobbyists and special interests also prompted reforms in campaign finance. While such concerns were not limited to the post-Watergate era—consider, for example, *The Douglas Subcommittee Report, Ethical Standards in Government* published in 1952 (Douglas, 1952)—the conditions of the time led to the passage of the Federal Election Campaign Act of 1971 and the Bipartisan Campaign Reform Act of 2002. These acts sought to limit the influence of special interests, particularly their campaign contributions.

Since the turn of the 21st century, we have seen remarkable advances in technology and an increased globalization of the economy. The growth of social media platforms, advances in digital technology and artificial intelligence, and the expansion of multinational corporations. These changes have heightened focus on issues related to transparency in government and the private sector. Advances in artificial intelligence, ranging from large language models to artificial general intelligence, pose significant pressures on the government to address the challenges our nation faces as this new technology evolves and becomes more widely adopted.

These concerns extend beyond national boundaries and impact national security interests. Despite ongoing efforts to combat corruption and ethical lapses by public officials, such problems are unlikely disappear entirely. New threats will inevitably emerge and require proactive measures to address them.

HOW ETHICAL CONDUCT OF MEMBERS IN GOVERNMENT IS MANAGED IN THE U.S.

As discussed earlier, the United States operates at three broad levels of government: federal, state, and local. Each level generally consists of an executive, legislative, and judicial branch. Due to the decentralized nature of this system, there is no single authority governing the ethical behavior of public servants. Here, the term "public servants" is used broadly to include civil service employees, appointed officials, and elected members of government. This section of the chapter provides a brief review of the recent history of how the federal government addresses ethics, followed by an even briefer discussion of how state and local governments manage ethics. While the previous section examined ethics from a philosophical and legal perspective, this section and the one that follows focus on practical application.

Before the 1970s, attempts to regulate the ethical behavior of public servants were largely decentralized, within individual agencies and departments managing their own ethical standards. However, the fallout from Watergate heightened mistrust in government among the electorate. According to the Pew Research Center (2015), trust in government peaked around 1964 at nearly 80%, but it fell sharply during the Vietnam War, civil unrest, and the Watergate scandal. Trust rebounded slightly during the Iranian hostage crisis and Ronald Reagan's presidency, dipped again during the Bush administration, and climbed briefly during Bill Clinton's presidency, peaking at 55% following the 9/11 terrorist attacks. Trust has since declined to its current level of around 19%.

In response to the erosion of trust in the wake of Watergate, President Jimmy Carter proposed an Ethics in Government Act in 1977. His proposal focused on three issues: (1) creating a financial disclosure program, (2) establishing an Office of Ethics in the Civil Service Commission, and (3) enhancing regulation of post-employment activities (The American Presidency Project, n.d.). Congress eventually passed the proposal as the Ethics in Government Act of 1978, PL 95-521 (U.S. Department of Justice, n.d.). The act required mandatory financial and employment history disclosures for public officials and their immediate families and imposed restrictions on post-employment lobbying activities. It also established the Office of Government Ethics (OGE) mentioned earlier, a special prosecutor, and a Senate legal counsel. This legislation marked the first significant step toward centralizing the regulation, monitoring, and enforcement of ethical standards for public servants (Strauss, 2023, May 30a).

Initially, the act focused on elected and appointed officials. Later, attention expanded to include civil service employees across the federal government. In February 1993, the OGE issued *Standards of Ethical Conduct for Employees of the Executive Branch* (5 C.F.R. Part 2635). These standards consist of eight subparts. The first subpart outlines general standards, concepts, and definitions, while the remaining subparts address specific areas of conduct, such as gifts, conflicts, impartiality, employment, misuse of position, and outside activities. These standards apply to over one million employees across 130 different agencies and departments, replacing the individual ethical codes previously in place within each executive agency and department (Strauss, 2023, May 30b).

In addition to the standards of ethics within the executive branch, the legislative and judicial branches also have their own mechanisms to manage the ethical conduct of their members. Since Congress is divided into two chambers, the House of Representatives (House) and Senate, each maintains its own standing committee to govern the ethics of its members. The House Committee on Ethics[2] and the Senate Select Committee on Ethics[3] are responsible for overseeing rules and standards of conduct, providing training, and addressing alleged violations. The judicial branch is overseen by a Committee on Codes of Conduct. The separation of powers among the branches necessitates that each manage its own affairs, including the ethical conduct of its members.

The House has an additional layer to assist in managing the ethics of its members: the Office of Congressional Ethics (OCE)[4]. Established in 2008, the OCE is an independent, nonpartisan organization tasked with reviewing and referring allegations of misbehavior by members of the House (Strauss, 2024). Members of the OCE are selected in equal numbers by leaders of the majority and minority

---

2   https://ethics.house.gov

3   https://ethics.senate.gov

4   https://oce.house.gov

parties. The OCE investigates alleged violations of laws, rules, regulations, or other standards of conduct by officers, members, or employees of the House. If the allegations are found credible, the matter may be referred to the House Ethics Committee for further action.

States also have mechanisms to oversee the conduct of public servants. Similar to the early stages of federal development, state mechanisms often focus on public servants who are elected or appointed to office rather than civil service employees working across the branches of state government. With fifty states, the powers and duties of these mechanisms vary significantly, making it beyond the scope of this chapter to explore them in detail. Instead, the objective is to make students aware of their existence and provide access to resources for learning about their own state. The National Conference of State Legislatures (NCSL) publishes a list of state ethics commissions along with brief descriptions of their functions (National Conference of State Legislatures, 2021, July 23).

As an example, we will briefly examine the State of Georgia (Department of Administrative Service, n.d.; Georgia.gov, n.d.). Georgia previously operated a State Ethics Commission, but the name was recently changed to more accurately reflect its role and duties. It is now known as the Georgia Government Transparency and Campaign Finance Commission. The day-to-day ethics of state employees are governed by a code of ethics issued by the Governor's Office and administered through the Department of Administrative Services. Adopted in 2021, the Code of Ethics requires employees to sign an attestation and regularly complete conflict-of-interest disclosures. The attestation confirms that the employee has received, read, and understood the code of ethics. Meanwhile, the Commission focuses on candidates, elected officials, donors, and lobbying.

How local governments manage the ethical climate within their jurisdiction is likely to vary by state and even within states (Demir et al., 2023). To illustrate this, we selected Atlanta, Georgia, because it is the state's largest city and one of the largest in the country. Larger cities are more likely to have a well-developed framework for managing the ethical climate than smaller cities across the state. Based on an examination of the city's website and historical records, Atlanta has maintained a code of ethics for all city employees since at least the mid-1980s (Atlanta Ethics, n.d.; Atlanta.gov, n.d., a; Atlanta.gov, n.d., b). The current code of ethics is divided into three major sections covering employees, elected officials, and board members.

In 2002 the Board of Ethics was "reconstituted," and an ethics officer appointed. In 2023 the Board's name was changed to the Governing Board of the Office of Inspector General and Ethics Office. The Board is responsible for ensuring compliance with the code of ethics and promoting an ethical culture throughout city government. It is composed of nine city residents nominated by private civic and professional organizations and appointed by the mayor and city council to serve three-year terms. While serving, board members are prohibited from engaging in partisan political activities or making campaign contributions.

This section provides a brief, though not comprehensive, overview of the mechanisms in place at the federal, state, and local levels for overseeing compliance with ethical codes of conduct and promoting an ethical climate within various government agencies and departments. Students interested in learning more can refer to the bibliography of this chapter as a starting point. To gain further insight into state and local ethics, consulting the websites of specific state or local governments is recommended.

The final section of this chapter will focus on an applied ethics situation and demonstrate the use of a basic ethical decision-making framework.

DESCRIBE A RELEVANT ETHICAL DECISION-MAKING MODEL AND ITS USE

As highlighted in earlier sections, public administration students have access to ample academic and practitioner literature to build a solid foundational knowledge of ethics within the discipline. While understanding ethics in public administration is intellectually important and engaging, its true value lies in the ability to apply this knowledge to real-life situations. Addressing an ethical dilemma in public administration requires a systematic and thoughtful approach.

We present such an approach below. This method is based on commonly-found ethical evaluation frameworks in textbooks across multiple disciplines. It is also possible that an organization may have a similar approach embedded in its policies and procedures for addressing ethical behavior. Public administration students should always follow the approach recommended by their organization.

The example provided here illustrates one such approach. It is followed by a hypothetical scenario demonstrating how it might be applied to a real ethical dilemma.

Table 7.2: Example Approach for Addressing an Ethical Dilemma

Action Step	Explanation
1. Recognize the Dilemma:	Identify and acknowledge that you are facing an ethical dilemma. This involves recognizing conflicting values, principles, or interests that require careful consideration.
2. Gather Information:	Collect all relevant facts and information related to the ethical dilemma. This includes understanding the context, stakeholders involved, potential consequences, and any relevant laws or regulations.
3. Identify Stakeholders:	Identify the stakeholders who may be affected by the decision. Consider the perspectives and interests of all parties involved, including those who may be directly or indirectly impacted.

Action Step	Explanation
4. Clarify Values and Principles:	Clearly articulate the values and ethical principles that are at stake. This may involve referring to established ethical guidelines, organizational codes of conduct, or broader ethical frameworks.
5. Consider Alternative Courses of Action:	Generate a list of possible courses of action that could be taken to address the ethical dilemma. Consider the advantages, disadvantages, and ethical implications of each alternative.
6. Evaluate Consequences:	Assess the potential consequences of each alternative. Consider short-term and long-term effects on stakeholders, the organization, and the broader community.
7. Apply Ethical Theories or Models:	If applicable, apply ethical theories or decision-making models (such as utilitarianism, deontology, or virtue ethics) to help analyze and justify the ethical implications of each course of action.
8. Consult with Colleagues or Superiors:	Seek input and advice from colleagues, superiors, or other relevant parties. Discussing the dilemma with others can provide additional perspectives and insights.
9. Review Organizational Policies and Legal Requirements:	Review organizational policies, codes of conduct, and legal requirements that may be relevant to the situation. Ensure that the proposed course of action aligns with these guidelines.
10. Decide:	Based on the information gathered and the analysis conducted, make an informed and ethically defensible decision. Choose the course of action that best aligns with ethical principles, organizational values, and legal requirements.
11. Communicate the Decision:	Clearly communicate the decision to relevant stakeholders. Provide transparent and honest communication about the reasons behind the decision and any steps that will be taken to address the ethical dilemma.
12. Reflect and Learn:	After the decision has been implemented, take time to reflect on the experience. Consider what was learned from the process and whether any adjustments can be made to prevent similar ethical dilemmas in the future.

It is important to note that ethical decision-making is an ongoing process. Public administrators should be prepared to reassess and adjust their approach as new information emerges or as circumstances evolve. Additionally, seeking guidance from ethical mentors or ethics committees within the organization can be invaluable when navigating complex ethical challenges.

Next, let us consider an example of an ethical dilemma in an anonymous U.S. city. This example focuses on a situation currently relevant to regional and local governments across the country: urban development and affordable housing. As I prepared to write this portion of the chapter, I was reminded of two situations from our region that involved development issues and the challenges people face in finding and maintaining affordable housing. Local administrators and elected officials were required to address these very real challenges, often without unanimous support from their respective communities.

Table 7.3: Scenario: Urban Development and Affordable Housing

Context:	Ethical Dilemma:
Imagine you are a city planner in a growing U.S. city facing increasing demand for housing due to population growth and economic development. The city is grappling with a shortage of affordable housing, and there is pressure to approve a new large-scale residential development project proposed by a private developer. The project promises to bring economic benefits, jobs, and increased tax revenue to the city.	The proposed development raises ethical concerns because it involves displacing a low-income community that currently resides in the project area. The new development would likely result in the eviction of existing residents, potentially leading to the loss of their homes, disruption of community ties, and increased housing costs for those who can't afford the new units.

Let us now walk through a set of practical steps—similar to those suggested earlier—for addressing this ethical dilemma:

Table 7.4: Addressing An Ethical Dilemma: An Example

Action Step	Explanation
1. Recognize the Dilemma:	Acknowledge that there is a conflict between the economic benefits of the development project and the potential harm to the existing low-income community.
2. Gather Information:	Collect data on the demographics of the affected community, housing affordability trends, and the projected impact of the development on the local housing market.
3. Identify Stakeholders:	Identify stakeholders, including current residents, the developer, local businesses, city officials, and advocacy groups focused on affordable housing.
4. Clarify Values and Principles:	Clearly articulate the values at stake, such as the right to housing, community well-being, and economic development.
5. Consider Alternative Courses of Action:	Explore alternative approaches, such as incentivizing mixed-income housing in the new development, providing relocation assistance for current residents, or finding alternative sites for the project.

Action Step	Explanation
6. Evaluate Consequences:	Assess the potential consequences of each alternative, considering the impact on housing affordability, community cohesion, and the overall well-being of residents.
7. Apply Ethical Theories or Models:	Apply ethical theories, such as utilitarianism (maximizing overall happiness) or principles of justice, to guide the decision-making process.
8. Consult with Colleagues or Superiors:	Seek input from colleagues, community leaders, and experts in urban development and affordable housing to gain diverse perspectives.
9. Review Organizational Policies and Legal Requirements:	Review city policies on affordable housing, zoning regulations, and any legal obligations related to community displacement.
10. Decide:	Make an informed decision that balances the need for economic development with the ethical obligation to protect the rights and well-being of existing residents.
11. Communicate the Decision:	Communicate the decision transparently to stakeholders, providing clear justifications and, if applicable, outlining any measures to mitigate the impact on the affected community.
12. Reflect and Learn:	Reflect on the decision-making process, gather feedback, and consider how the city can improve its approach to balancing economic development and social equity in future projects.

In this scenario, the ethical dilemma involves balancing the tension between economic development and the well-being of a vulnerable community. The practical steps emphasize a comprehensive and inclusive decision-making process that considers the interests and values of all stakeholders. This approach is crucial because it is unlikely that any decision will satisfy all stakeholders. However, a careful and systematic process will be easier to explain and defend, particularly when facing pressure from those stakeholders who are least satisfied with the outcome. Moreover, this approach is more likely to result in a decision that provides relief to those most affected by its impact.

EXPLAIN THE ETHICAL CHALLENGES PRESENT IN THE 21ST CENTURY

The 21st century brings changes and developments that will pose unique ethical challenges for public administrators. These include technological advances and cybersecurity issues, shifting demographics and diversity, increased globalization with implications for intergovernmental relations, environmental sustainability and climate change, and budgetary constraints challenging fiscal responsibility. Public administrators must be prepared to navigate these changes and address any new or unique ethical dilemmas they present in crafting and implementing policies.

The ethical implications of advances in technology and cybersecurity center on the responsible development and use of emerging technologies, such as increasing availability of artificial intelligence (AI). Public administrators will need to issues such as protecting privacy rights, preventing the misuse of data, and safeguarding organizations and individuals from cyber threats. Challenges include enhanced surveillance capabilities, the risks of hacking and data breaches, and the potential misuse of AI across society. These significant challenges are likely to cause some administrators many sleepless nights.

As an example of how AI is impacting society, two executive orders have been issued in recent years to address its potential impacts, both positive and negative. Executive Order 13960, issued on December 8, 2020, encourages federal agencies to explore responsible ways to implement AI. EO 14110, issued on October 30, 2023, aims to protect Americans from the potential risks associated with AI development and adoption. It is worth a students' time to read both orders and reflect on how AI might influence policies and procedures at all levels of government.

Ethical challenges arising from demographic changes will focus on diversity, equity, and inclusion. Public administrators must consider fair representation in employment, the impact of policy decisions, the prevention of discrimination, and the development of policies that reflect the diverse makeup of the population. Ensuring that public organizations are representative of the populations they serve and that policies account for diversity will require ethical leadership.

Examples of demographic diversity include the growing Latino population, issues related to immigration and naturalization policies, LGBTQ+ rights and equal protection laws, and ongoing race relation issues affecting Black Americans, such as those involving law enforcement and the legal system. Addressing these challenges will be critical in fostering equity and trust within public administration.

Ethical implications are often intertwined with the globalization of politics and the economy, even if not immediately evident. The globalization of our economy requires public organizations to navigate intergovernmental relations more effectively. Key issues include sovereignty, fairness in international agreements and treaties, and addressing global challenges in an equitable manner. Public administrators at all levels of government must be capable of addressing the ethical dimensions of international cooperation and crafting diplomatic and economic policies that benefit not only their own jurisdiction but also contribute to overall global well-being.

The COVID-19 pandemic highlighted the ethical complexities of global and national public health challenges, many of which will likely persist into the future. A prime example is the development and distribution of vaccines for highly communicable and potentially deadly viruses. Pandemics pose ethical challenges in emergency management and crisis communications. Public administrators and elected leaders must ensure fair and just outcomes in areas such as sharing pandemic response strategies, providing treatment for those infected, and ensuring equitable access to vaccines to curb the spread of disease. Public health crises raise ethical considerations across many facets of public administration.

Environmental sustainability is another critical issue, frequently highlighted in news stories about the impacts of climate change on the nation and the world. As resource constraints become more apparent and the effects of human behavior are better understood, public administrators face growing challenges. These include responsibility for environmental degradation, eroding ecosystems, rising temperatures, and increasingly severe weather events. Decision-making must balance economic development with ecological preservation and consider the rights of current and future generations to enjoy a healthy environment.

REFERENCES

Adams, J. (1798). From John Adams to Massachusetts Militia, 11 October 1798 [Letter]. *Founders online*. National Archives. https://founders.archives.gov/documents/Adams/99-02-02-3102.

Appleby, P. H. (1952) *Morality and administration in democratic government* (p. 13). Baton Rouge: Louisiana State University Press.

Atlanta Ethics. (n.d.). *Integrity matters: Welcome to Atlanta ethics*. Retrieved December 22, 2023, from https://www.atlantaethics.org/

City of Atlanta, GA. (n.d.). Governing board of the office of the inspector general and ethics office. Atlantaga.gov. Retrieved December 22, 2023, from https://www.atlantaga.gov/government/board-of-ethics

City of Atlanta, GA. (n.d., -b). Standards of conduct. Atlantaga.gov. https://www.atlantaga.gov/government/boards-and-commissions/submit-application-to-be-on-a-board/view-this-code-of-ethics/ethical-guidelines-for-employees

Behn, R. D. (2001). *Rethinking democratic accountability*. Brookings Institute Press.

Cohen, S., & Eimicke, W. B. (1995). Ethics and the public administrator. *The Annals of the American Academy of Political and Social Science, 537*, 96–108. http://www.jstor.org/stable/1047757

Congressional Research Service. (n.d.) *Constitution of the United States: Analysis and interpretation*. Retrieved November 11, 2023, from https://constitution.congress.gov/browse/essay/intro.8-6/ALDE_00001307/

Verschoor, C. C. (2016, May 2). The importance of trust. *Strategic finance*, Institute of Management Accountants.

Demir, T., Reddick, C. G., & Perlman, B. J. (2023). In search of ethics infrastructure in US local governments: Building blocks or dead end? *Administration & Society, 55*(10), 1866-1892.

Department of Administrative Services. (n.d.). *Governor's code of ethics*. Retrieved December 21, 2023, from https://doas.ga.gov/human-resources-administration/

governors-code-ethics

Douglas, P. H. (1952). Improvement of ethical standards in the federal government: problems and proposals. *The Annals of the American Academy of Political and Social Science, 280*(1), 149–157.

Eizenstat, S. E. (2018). *Inspectors general 40th anniversary speech: The general context for inspectors general*. Retrieved May 3, 2024, from https://www.ignet.gov/sites/default/files/files/40th_Commemoration_Stuart_Eizenstat_Speech.pdf

Frederickson, H. G. (1997). *The spirit of public administration*. Jossey-Bass.

Frederickson, H. G. & Ghere, R. K. (2013). Ethics in public management. *Political Science Faculty Publications* (Publication No. 43). https://ecommons.udayton.edu/pol_fac_pub/43

Georgia.gov. (n.d.). *State ethics commission*. Retrieved December 21, 2023, from https://georgia.gov/organization/georgia-government-transparency-campaign-finance-commission

Grannan, C. (2023, June 8). What's the difference between morality and ethics? *Encyclopedia britannica*. https://www.britannica.com/story/whats-the-difference-between-morality-and-ethics.

Heath, J. (2020). A general framework for the ethics of public administration. *The Machinery of Government: Public Administration and the Liberal State* (online ed.). Oxford Academic. https://doi.org/10.1093/oso/9780197509616.003.0002

Ingraham, P. W. (1995). *The foundation of merit: Public service in American democracy*. The Johns Hopkins University Press.

Lawrence v. Texas, 539 U.S. 558 (2003). Retrieved from https://oconnorlibrary.org/supreme-court/lawrence-v-texas-2002

Locke, H. G. (1995). Ethics in American government: A look backward. *The Annals of the American Academy of Political and Social Science, 537*, 14–24. http://www.jstor.org/stable/1047751

Markkula Center for Applied Ethics. (n.d.). What is government ethics? *Markkula Center for Applied Ethics at Santa Clara University*. Retrieved May 3, 2024, from https://www.scu.edu/government-ethics/resources/what-is-government-ethics/

Merriam-Webster. (n.d.). Ethic. In *Merriam-Webster.com dictionary*. Retrieved May 3, 2024, from https://www.merriam-webster.com/dictionary/ethic

National Conference of State Legislatures. (2021, July 23). *State Ethics Commissions: Powers and Duties*. Retrieved December 21, 2023, from https://www.ncsl.org/ethics/state-ethics-commissions-powers-and-duties

Office of Congressional Ethics. (n.d.). Retrieved December 21, 2023, from https://oce.house.gov/

Open AI. (2024). *ChatGPT* (May 3 version) [Large language model]. https://chat.openai.com/chat

Pew Research Center. (2015, November 23). Beyond distrust: How Americans view their government. Retrieved December 21, 2023, from https://www.pewresearch.org/politics/2015/11/23/1-trust-in-government-1958-2015/

Richardson, W. D., & Nigro, L. G. (1987). Administrative ethics and founding thought: Constitutional correctives, honor, and education. *Public Administration Review*, *47*(5), 367–376. https://doi.org/10.2307/976061

Shafritz, J. M. (2004). Ethics. In *The dictionary of public policy and administration* (p. 106). Westview Press.

Singer, P. (2023, October 29). Ethics. *Encyclopedia britannica*. https://www.britannica.com/topic/ethics-philosophy

Standards of Ethical Conduct for Employees of the Executive Branch, 5 C.F.R. Part 2635. (2022). Retrieved from https://www.ecfr.gov/current/title-5/chapter-XVI/subchapter-B/part-2635#part-2635

Strauss, J. R. (2023, March 31). *Senate select committee on ethics: A brief history of its evolution and jurisdiction.* (CRS Report No. RL30650). Retrieved from https://crsreports.congress.gov/product/pdf/RL/RL30650

Strauss, J. R. (2023, May 30a). *Executive branch ethics and financial disclosure administration: The role of designated agency ethics officials.* (CRS Report No. IF12019). https://crsreports.congress.gov/product/pdf/IF/IF12019

Strauss, J. R. (2023, May 30b). *Office of government ethics: A primer.* (CRS Report No. IF 10634). Retrieved from https://crsreports.congress.gov/product/pdf/IF/IF10634

Strauss, J. R. (2024, February 28). *House office of congressional ethics: History, authority, and procedures.* (CRS Report No. R40760). Retrieved from https://crsreports.congress.gov/product/pdf/R/R40760

Svara, J. H. (2014). Who are the keepers of the Ccde? Articulating and upholding ethical standards in the field of public administration. *Public Administration Review*, *74*(5), 561–569. http://www.jstor.org/stable/24029399

The American Presidency Project. (n.d.). Ethics in government message to the Congress. Retrieved December 21, 2023, from https://www.presidency.ucsb.edu/documents/ethics-government-message-the-congress

U.S. Department of Justice. (n.d.-a). *Summary – Executive branch standards of ethical conduct.* Retrieved December 21, 2023, from https://www.justice.gov/jmd/ethics/principles-ethical-conduct

U.S. Department of Justice. (n.d.-b). *Ethics in Government Act of 1978 – Public Law 95-521, October 26, 1978.* Retrieved December 21, 2023, from https://www.ojp.gov/ncjrs/virtual-library/abstracts/ethics-government-act-1978-public-law-95-521-october-26-1978

U.S. Office of Government Ethics. (n.d.). *Our history.* Retrieved May 3, 2024, from https://www.oge.gov/web/oge.nsf/about_our-history

U.S. Senate Select Committee on Ethics. (n.d.). Retrieved on December 21, 2023, from https://www.ethics.senate.gov/public/

U.S. House of Representatives Committee on Ethics. (n.d.). Retrieved December 21, 2023, from https://ethics.house.gov/

Watergate: Its Implications for Responsible Government. (1974). *Administration & Society*, 6(2), 155–170. https://doi.org/10.1177/009539977400600201

Efficiency and Effectiveness in Public Administration

LEARNING OBJECTIVES

Students studying this chapter should be able to:

1. Define the terms efficiency and effectiveness.
2. Summarize the origins of efficiency and effectiveness as management concepts.
3. Describe how they are integrated into the study and practice of public administration.
4. Integrate these concepts with the broader study of leadership.

INTRODUCTION

Efficiency and effectiveness are qualities that repeatedly show up in discussions about public administration, with roots extending far back in history. As you may recall from chapter one, business management and public administration share some principles, concepts, and qualities while differing in others. The concern with efficiency and effectiveness is one of the common connections between these two fields.

Public administrators frequently face pressures on both the input and output sides of functions and programs. Constituents often criticize how much they are required to contribute to the running of government, while also expressing concern over how the financial resources are used. This puts those serving in the public sector in what can feel like a no-win situation. This pressure on public administrators is often to do more with less. At the same time, the menu of outputs is scrutinized and criticized, leaving public administrators to make difficult decisions.

Rainey (2014) illustrates this point by referencing a study of police chiefs conducted by Moore (1990). He writes, "Police chiefs must try to find a balance between keeping the peace, enforcing the law, controlling crime, preventing crime, ensuring fairness and respect for citizen rights, and operating efficiently and with minimal costs" (Rainey 2014 p. 152).

This chapter will briefly examine the qualities of efficiency and effectiveness as they relate to public administration and will attempt to connect them to other qualities, including value, economy, and compliance. It is important for leaders in the public sector to consider these qualities in the decision-making process.

DEFINING EFFICIENCY AND EFFECTIVENESS

Efficiency and effectiveness are different but related qualities. *Merriam-Webster* (p. 397) defines "efficiency" as "the quality or degree of being efficient," while the word "efficient" is defined as "being or involving the immediate agent in producing an effect." It is further described as being productive without waste. "Effectiveness" (p. 397) is listed as the noun form of "effective," and is defined as "producing a decided, decisive, or desired effect." In their explanation of "effective," *Merriam-Webster* includes a note referring to "efficient" as a synonym, stating it "suggests an acting or a potential for action or use in such a way as to avoid loss or waste."

Based on these definitions, efficiency can be described as a function of inputs versus outputs, measuring the use of inputs per output to assess resource usage. Effectiveness, on the other hand, focuses more on goals and objectives. It is a function of outcomes: did the program or organization meet the stated goals and objectives?

The two qualities can operate in conjunction, achieving desired outcomes while consuming a minimum or optimal level of resources, or they can work inversely— where outcomes are achieved but at the expense of higher resource usage. The opposite is also true, where goals may not be met but fewer resources are used. Efficiency and effectiveness are related but independent of each other.

ORIGIN OF EFFICIENCY AND EFFECTIVENESS

To better understand the qualities of efficiency and effectiveness, we will examine the origins of these two terms. The term "efficiency" has roots reaching back to the philosophy of Aristotle. The Greek phrase *arche tes metabolis* translates to "origin of change," which was later interpreted as efficiency. This was one of the four causes of change identified by Aristotle and is closely associated with the Latin phrase *causa efficiens*, meaning "producing or causing an effect." It was not until the Enlightenment and the Industrial Revolution that the term evolved from a qualitative description of the cause of change to a quantitative concept focused on the use of resources to achieve some outcome. Today, "efficiency" refers to a ratio of inputs to outputs rather the agent or cause of change.

The term "effectiveness" derives from the Latin *effectivus*, meaning "productive," and *efficere*, meaning "to accomplish" or "to bring about." The Greek words *telos* (end or purpose) and *arete* (excellence or virtue) also contribute to this concept, which refers to the ability of actions to achieve a desired outcome or goal. Machiavelli (1513) discussed effectiveness in terms of a ruler's ability to achieve and maintain power (goal or objective). The modern definition of effectiveness emerged during the the Scientific and Industrial Revolutions, when it came to signify the ability to produce reliable and replicable results. During this period, efficiency also became linked to effectiveness due to a focus on resource usage in achieving desired results.

Our modern understanding of efficiency and effectiveness is also shaped by the management theory literature. Theorists such as Henri Fayol, Max Weber, and Chester Barnard made significant contributions to these concepts. Their work helped develop management theory and practice, embedding the constructs of efficiency and effectiveness into the field. These ideas also influenced the development of modern public administration in the United States and abroad, a topic we will explore in the next section.

Heni Fayol (1841–1925) focused his work on three primary areas: (1) administrative theory, (2) principles of management, and (3) a concept known as the scalar chain. His administrative theory emphasized applying management principles to various types of organizations. Fayol identified five key functions of management—planning, organizing, commanding, coordinating, and controlling—which serve as a framework for understanding the role of management within an organization. Additionally, he proposed fourteen principles of management:

1. Division of work

2. Authority and responsibility

3. Discipline

4. Unity of command

5. Unity of direction

6. Alignment of interest

7. Remuneration of employees

8. Centralization

9. Scalar chain

10. Order

11. Equity

12. Stability of personnel

13. Initiative

14. Esprit de corps

The functions and principles proposed by Fayol influenced later developments in management and administration. Notably, they informed the work of President Roosevelt's Brownlow Committee, which introduced the now-famous acronym POSDCORB: planning, organizing, staffing, directing, coordinating, reporting, and budgeting. The scalar chain, listed as principle nine above, reflects Fayol's ideas on the chain of command, emphasizing the need for clear and transparent lines of communication across various levels of an organization.

Max Weber, a German theorist who lived from 1864 to 1920, wrote extensively on management theory practice, and organizational structure. His works, originally written in German, were not translated and published in English until after his death. One notable publication, *Economy and Society*, was released in English in 1922, nearly two years posthumously. Weber's ideas significantly shaped our understanding of management and bureaucracy. He argued that bureaucracy is a rational and efficient form of organization, characterized by division of labor, hierarchy of authority, rules and regulations, impersonality, and career advancement based on merit.

Chester Barnard, an American theorist (1886–1961), began his career in industry and became president of New Jersey Bell Telephone in 1927. His first major contribution to management literature, *The Functions of the Executive*, was published in 1938. Barnard identified three critical functions: communications, planning, and coordinating/controlling. He recognized the importance of identifying organizational goals and objectives, communicating them throughout the organization, and managing people to ensure alignment with these goals and objectives. Barnard also explored the concept of an informal organization existing within a formal organization, emphasizing the influence of internal networks in organization and their importance to their organizational success. Much of this work is evident today in the formation of affinity or resource groups in many large organizations, centered on identities such as race, nationality, and sexual orientation.

The work of Fayol, Weber, and Barnard contributed significantly to organization and management theory, particularly in relation to efficiency and effectiveness. Their theories focused on optimizing organizational success through the efficient use of resources (both human and financial) and effective communication via formal and informal channels. While these three individuals were instrumental in advancing management theory, they are among many contributors who have influenced our understanding of the theory and practice of management and contributed to our understanding of the qualities of efficiency and effectiveness in organizational contexts.

INTEGRATING EFFICIENCY AND EFFECTIVENESS OF PUBLIC ADMINISTRATION

The integration of the qualities of efficiency and effectiveness into public administration is largely attributable to work published during the late 19th and early 20th centuries. This area of research, theory, and practice aligns closely with the broader field of management (some aspects of which were discussed in the previous section). Concerns over efficiency and effectiveness in public administration initially stemmed from a patron-based system to one based on merit. The development of the civil service redirected attention to selecting, training, and retaining staff with the skills necessary to perform required functions, rather than basing employment on party and candidate loyalty. Ingraham (1995) observes that "neutral competence would exclude politics; decision would be rational, and resources could be used for maximum efficiency." The evolution of public employment into a merit-based system revealed efficiency as "one of many objectives pursued by governmental agencies."

Between the 1890s and 1912, Frederick Taylor presented his work on scientific management, which significantly influenced public administration.

While Taylor did not explicitly intend for scientific management to address efficiency, it certainly did so indirectly. In testimony before Congress (1912), Taylor stated that scientific management "is not any efficiency device . . . " but instead described it as "a complete mental revolution on the part of the workingman engaged in any particular establishment or industry . . . " Despite his intentions, the result of scientific management was an enhanced focus on efficiency and effectiveness, translating into a heightened focus on time, cost, revenue, and profit—maximizing revenue and profit at the lowest possible cost. This was evident later in his testimony when he remarked, "it is, I think, safe and conservative to say that output of the individual workman has been, on average, doubled."

Locke (1982) does a nice job summarizing the major components of Taylor's *Principles of Scientific Management* (1911). The mindset change Taylor describes in his writings and testimony was achieved through various methods and techniques. He indirectly addressed efficiency and effectiveness in the workplace through the following principles: Taylor advocated for standardizing processes, by defining tasks in the incremental steps necessary to complete them. He recommended time and motion studies to standardize work processes further. He also recommended the division of labor, allowing individuals to specialize rather than requiring everyone to act as generalists, a principle similar to one promoted earlier by Adam Smith.

Taylor argued for the importance of properly training individuals to perform their assigned tasks, asserting that efficiency arises from developing proficiency at completing a specific job. To boost productivity, he recommended incentive systems and a hierarchical structure with clear lines of authority to ensure tasks were performed correctly. Additionally, Taylor promoted the value of continuous improvement, regularly evaluating performance to ensure standards were met.

Around the same time, a future U.S. president began an academic career focused on public administration. In 1887, Woodrow Wilson published an article often regarded as the first significant contribution to public administration in the United States. Wilson posited that administration is a science and related it to management. In the opening paragraph, he asserted, "civil service reform must, after the accomplishment of its first purpose, expand into efforts to improve, not the personnel only, but also the organization and methods of our government offices." He further stated, "The object of administrative study to discover first, what government can properly do, and, secondly, how it can do these proper things with the utmost possible efficiency and at the least possible cost either of money or energy."

In his essay, Wilson outlines the keys to achieving these objectives. The first is employing specialization in administrative tasks. Second, closely related to specialization, is developing expertise in specific administrative areas. Third, Wilson focused on streamlining administrative operations to simplify processes and eliminate redundancies. He also upholds the civil service system as a significant improvement over political patronage, because filling government positions based on competence and qualifications fosters an environment focused on specialization and expertise. While not explicitly stated, all these principles or qualities reflect a focus on efficiency, as noted in the opening paragraph of Wilson's paper, as well as effectiveness in achieving the government's administrative and programmatic goals and objectives.

Discussions on the qualities of efficiency and effectiveness are not limited to the late 19th and early 20th centuries. More recent theorists and practitioners have expanded the public administration literature referencing these qualities. Frederickson (1997) observes that "efficiency and economy have long been the twin pillars of theory." He explains efficiency as achieving as much public good as available resources allow, while economy focuses on minimizing the use of financial resources. Frederickson also argues for the addition of a third pillar to address the government's role in satisfying citizens' needs. This third pillar, which he refers to as social equity, is in some ways equivalent to effectiveness, as fulfilling citizens' needs aligns with the goal of achieving effectiveness in government.

Herbert Simon (1978, 1997) also wrote extensively about efficiency, noting the shift in its definition from a focus on achieving results through effort to more of a measurement-based approach, emphasizing the ratio of inputs to outputs. In *Administrative Behavior* (1997), Simon states, "The criterion of efficiency dictates that choice of alternatives which produces the largest results for the given application of resources" (p. 256). Simon does a nice job in chapter nine of *Administrative Behavior* laying out the theory and criticisms of efficiency. Focusing on it as one of the three criteria often considered foundational to public administration (effectiveness, efficiency, and economy), Simon emphasizes the importance of stating goals and objectives in a quantifiable manner to facilitate assessment. In his conclusion to the chapter, Simon states that efficiency "requires that results be maximized with limited resources."

He also devotes significant writing space to the challenges of distinguishing between the factual versus value-based nature of goals and objectives, noting the difficulties in assessing efficiency if goals are value-based. This criticism will surface in more recent academic writing about the foundation of public administration.

During the period spanning the 1960s to 2000s, public administration saw the rise of two schools of thought: new public management (NPM) and reinventing government. To summarize the new public management movement, we reference writings by Christopher Hood (1991, 1995). Hood identifies seven doctrinal components of new public management (paraphrased as follows): (1) decentralization, (2) contracting, (3) privatization, (4) efficiency, (5) discretion, (6) accountability, and (7) results. The three most relevant to our examination of efficiency include the focus on what Hood labels as frugality, which he argues places more emphasis on the bottom line; accountability, which he ties to measurable performance indicators and the use of audits; and outputs, which he explains as a shift in focus from detailed accounting to broader cost center accounting. From new public management, we can see the relative importance of efficiency, as noted from the discussion on inputs, outputs, and measurability.

Another framework introduced during this same period was referred to as "reinventing government" (Osborne & Gaebler, 1992). Like new public management, the "reinventing government" movement shifted focus to goal achievement (outputs and outcomes) but did not completely abandon concern for efficiency. The key points related to efficiency in this movement included separating strategic from operating decision-making, shifting services (operations) to the private sector, increasing community participation in finding efficient solutions, increasing the use of competition in service provision, focusing on mission and results, and paying greater attention to citizen (customer) preferences. This market-based orientation, the authors argued, would lead to both greater effectiveness and efficiency. Osborne followed this book with two others (1997, 2004), further advancing these ideas while focusing on the importance of balancing budgets to control finances and reducing reliance on traditional forms of bureaucracy (Frederickson, 1996).

INTEGRATING EFFICIENCY WITH LEADERSHIP

The shift in focus toward effectiveness in achieving goals or objectives has also been discussed in the management literature. Simon (1997) referenced the work of Peter Drucker in *Administrative Behavior*. Drucker coined the phrase "management by objectives," focusing on setting clear and measurable goals. He struck a balance between efficiency and effectiveness in his writing, describing efficiency as "doing things right" and effectiveness as "doing the right things." Drucker's core principles mirrored those in NPM and "reinventing government," including a focus on decentralization, investment in training and development, and customer preferences. In the past twenty-five years, the literature on public administration has increasingly paid attention to the importance of values in public organizations, complicating any straightforward consideration of efficiency.

Manzoor (2014) states, "Efficiency takes on a whole new perspective when we try to study it in an environment of traditionally measured quantities in a system that is heavily based on values, inspirations, and human perceptions." He contrasts traditional rational bureaucratic organizations with those that "pursue multiple value-based goals in a democratic system." Manzoor argues that measuring efficiency in such public organizations is more challenging than in private organizations. However, Simon (1997) also notes that measuring efficiency in private organizations is not always straightforward, positing that profitability ratios fail to capture the value-based objectives in private organizations just as they do in public ones.

Meyer et al. (2022) more recently proposed an alternative set of pillars for public administration theory: (1) empathy, (2) engagement, (3) equity, and (4) ethics, as opposed to the traditional economy, efficiency, and effectiveness. They summarize the three traditional pillars in Table 1 (p. 354) of their text, describing economy as the management of scarce resources, efficiency as achieving the greatest outcome for the fewest resources, and effectiveness as how well an organization accomplishes its work. Their new framework takes account people's feelings, direct public contact, fairness, and justice, and a moral code guiding professional behavior. The authors pose the following question: What is the role of public administration in a post-COVID-19 pandemic world? They argue that a shift from traditional pillars to a modified framework is necessary to build the knowledge and skills needed to address today's wicked problems.

Rainey (2014) discusses the balanced scorecard for goal setting and assessment, introduced by Kaplan and Norton (1996). The balanced scorecard categorizes goals and objectives, along with their related measures, into four perspectives: (1) financial perspective, (2) customer perspective, (3) internal perspective, and (4) learning and growth perspective. This aligns with the National Performance Review introduced in the 1990s, focusing an organization's strategic and operational planning on key aspects of its mission. The balanced scorecard blends the scientific management definition of efficiency with a more modern values-based mission perspective.

Students reading this chapter should recognize that while efficiency is a necessary concept for assessing performance, it remains difficult to define and measure due to the complex nature of missions and related strategic plan goals and objectives. We encourage students to explore this topic further, as the literature continues to produce additional thinking on it both in public administration and, more generally, the management literature.

CONCLUSION

This chapter provides an overview of the concept of efficiency, its definition, how it is integrated into public administration, and more generally into leadership. Originally, the word "efficiency" focused on the idea of effort applied to accomplish a goal or objective. Over time, as science and technology evolved, the focus shifted toward a more technical or mechanistic view. Innovation led to the definition of efficiency becoming more about the relationship between inputs and outputs—a ratio that could be used to assess performance over time and across organizations, programs, or individuals.

Academics and practitioners continue to critique and evaluate the definition and application of efficiency. The latter half of the 20th century and the first quarter of the 21st century have seen further change in how efficiency is understood, as theorists and practitioners increasingly acknowledge the multi-faceted nature of missions and goals, which include both factual and value-based components. What we have learned from this chapter is that efficiency is not an easy concept to define or measure, but it will remain an important pillar of public administration and an important consideration for leaders.

REFERENCES

Bulletin of the Taylor Society. (1926). Testimony of Frederick W. Taylor at hearings before Special Committee of the House of Representatives, January 1912: A classic of management literature reprinted, in full, from a rare public document. *Bulletin of the Taylor Society, 11*(3–4), 95-196. New York, New York: The Taylor Society.

Denhardt, J. V. & Denhardt, R. B. (2007). *The new public service: Serving, not steering.* M.E. Sharpe.

Florina, P. (2017). Elements on the efficiency and effectiveness of the public sector. *Ovidius University Annals, Series Economic Sciences, 17*(2), 313.

Frederickson, H. G. (1996). Comparing the Reinventing Government Movement with the New Public Administration. *Public Administration Review, 56*(3), 263–270. https://doi.org/10.2307/976450

Frederickson, G. H. (1997). *The spirit of public administration.* Jossey-Bass.

Hood, C. (1991). A public management for all seasons? *Public Administration, 69*(1), 3–19. https://doi.org/10.1111/j.1467-9299.1991.tb00779.x

Hood, C. (1995). The "New Public Management" in the 1980's: Variations on a theme. *Accounting, Organizations, and Society, 20*(2–3), 93–109.

Ingraham, P. W. (1995). *The foundation of merit: Public service in American democracy.* Johns Hopkins University Press.

Locke, E. A. (1982). The ideas of Frederick W. Taylor: An evaluation. *The Academy of Management Review, 7*(1), 14–24.

Manzoor, A. (2014). A look at efficiency in public administration: Past and future. *Sage Open, 4*(4). https://doi.org/10.1177/2158244014564936

Meyer, S. J., Johnson, R. G., & McCandless, S. (2022). Meet the new Es: Empathy, engagement, equity, and ethics in public administration. *Public Integrity, 24*(4–5), 353–363. https://doi.org/10.1080/10999922.2022.2074764

Online Etymology Dictionary. (n.d.). Search for efficiency, retrieved May 15, 2024, from https://etymonline.com

Online Etymology Dictionary. (n.d.). Search for effectiveness, retrieved May 15, 2024, from https://etymonline.com

OpenAI. (2024). *ChatGPT* (May 14 version) [Large language model]. https://chat.openai.com

OpenAI. (2024). *ChatGPT* (May 16 version) [Large language model]. https://chat.openai.com

Osborne, D., & Gaebler T. (1992). *Reinventing government: How the entrepreneurial spirit is transforming the public sector from school house to state house, city hall to the Pentagon*. Addison Wesley.

Osborne, D., & Hutchinson, P. (2004). *The price of government: Getting the results we need in an age of permanent fiscal crisis*. Basic Books.

Osborne, D., & Plastrik, P. (1997). *Banishing bureaucracy: The five strategies for reinventing government*. Addison Wesley.

Person, H. S. (1926). Significance of the investigation: The Management Movement–Taylor's contribution–Why it stimulated investigation–What the investigation brought out. *Bulletin of the Taylor Society, 11*(3–4), 90–94, 196. The Taylor Society.

Rainey, H. G. (2014). *Understanding and managing public organizations* (5th ed.). Jossey-Bass.

Ridley, C. E., & Simon, H. A. (1938). The criterion of efficiency. *The Annals of the American Academy of Political and Social Science, 199*(1), 20–25.

Rutgers, M. R., & van der Meer, H. (2010). The origins of efficiency in public administration: Regaining efficiency as the core value of public administration. *Administration & Society, 42*(7), 755–779.

Shafritz, J. M., Hyde, A. C., & Parkes, S. J. (2004). *Classics of public administration* (5th ed.). Wadsworth/Thomson Learning.

Simon, H. A. (1978). Rationality as process and as product of thought. *The American Economic Review, 68*(2), 1–16.

Simon, H. A. (1997) *Administrative behavior: A study of decision-making processes in administrative organizations* (4th ed.). Free Press.

Taylor, F. W. (1915). *The principles of scientific management*. Harper & Brothers Publishers.

Wilson, W. (1887). The Study of Administration. *Political Science Quarterly, 2*, 197–222.

Public Financial Management

LEARNING OBJECTIVES

Students studying this chapter should be able to:

1. Define public financial management and its importance in public administration.
2. Summarize, in general terms, the public financial management process.
3. Identify the two major legislative actions affecting the federal budget process.
4. Briefly explain the federal budget process as it operates today.
5. Briefly describe Georgia's and Atlanta's budgetary process.
6. Discuss accounting reporting and controls.

INTRODUCTION

One of the final topics we address in this text is the management of public financial resources. With financial resources, what was discussed in earlier chapters becomes possible. This makes the topic of this chapter critically important for all students studying public administration and aspiring to leadership roles in public organizations.

All leaders and managers in government need to be familiar with financial management, because all their decisions will have a financial impact on the government. These decisions may involve personnel, operating policies and procedures, managing capital assets, and investing of financial resources—all necessary for the government to meet its mission.

Unlike private businesses that raise financial resources through the sale of products and services or not-for-profit organizations that rely on donations and grants, governments raise financial resources predominantly through taxes and fees levied on citizens. This method of raising financial resources leads to higher scrutiny of how those resources are used.

Therefore, managers and leaders in government must be capable of assessing the potential financial impact of their decisions before implementing them, to avoid critical mistakes that could result in negative financial consequences. This chapter is a brief introduction to public financial management, intended to spark interest and encourage students to take a deeper look into this important topic.

DEFINE PUBLIC FINANCIAL MANAGEMENT ITS IMPORTANCE

What is public financial management, and why is it important? We will address the first question before tackling the second. Generally, like all financial management, public financial management consists of the processes, systems, and institutions necessary to plan, budget, raise, spend, and account for financial resources (USAID, n.d.). According to Miller (1991), "Financial managers act much the same as all other managers: both try to reduce ambiguity that comes with uncertain sources and amounts of resources; both act by aligning the demands of critical outside interests or contingencies with the capabilities and interests of organization members" (p. 1).

Individuals working in public administration must focus on the effective, efficient, and economical use of the government's financial resources to meet the needs of the community they serve and achieve the strategic and operating objectives of the government, whether at the federal, state, or local level. Miller (1991) further notes that "the centrality of resource acquisition and allocation makes the financial manager a critical, even pivotal, actor in organization life" (p. 2)

Public financial management is a broad topic that includes several key components: budgeting, financial accounting, and monitoring. The budgeting cycle encompasses three primary phases: formulation, execution, and monitoring (Jordan and Hackbart, 2022; Willoughby and Jensen, 2022). Financial accounting involves managing revenue and expenditure cycles, along with periodic financial reporting (Johnson and Abbas, 2022; Ross and Duncan, 2022). Monitoring includes internal and external monitoring activities, such as an annual independent financial audit (Gabrini, 2022).

An effectively-designed public financial management system also includes internal controls to safeguard government resources against fraud, waste, and abuse, while ensuring accurate financial reporting. Among the various aspects of public financial management, budgeting plays a particularly crucial role and is a central feature of the discipline. According to Harold Smith (1944), a former director of the U.S. Bureau of the Budget (Appleby, 1947), "budgeting is not only a central function but a process that should permeate the entire administrative structure."

Throughout this text, our focus has been on public administration as practiced in the United States. We have primarily addressed its practice at the federal level but have also included discussions on state and local government. This chapter continues in that vein.

To explain the importance of public financial management, it is helpful to consider the demands placed on government at all levels. At the federal level (United States Treasury, n.d.), the government must meet the needs of mandatory programs such as Social Security, Medicare, Medicaid, and other programs referred to as entitlement programs. In addition, there is a long list of discretionary programs and policy areas, including national defense, education, health and human services, veterans' affairs, housing and urban development, transportation, environment, homeland security, space, and international affairs. The federal government must also finance the national debt, making regular interest payments and paying down the principal on borrowed funds.

State governments have their own finances to manage (Urban Institute, n.d.). These include meeting the needs of educating their citizens by overseeing K-12 education and higher education systems. States also manage health and human services, such as Medicaid and social services, and addressing major policy areas like transportation (infrastructure, highways, and public transit), public safety (police, fire, and emergency management), corrections (courts and prisons), and general government operations. Like the federal level, state governments must also manage their debt by making periodic interest payments and paying down principal.

Meanwhile, local governments must manage a wide range of programs and policy areas, some unique and others overlapping with those at the state and federal levels (Urban Institute, n.d.). Local governments, which include counties, cities, and special purpose entities, oversee local school systems; operate fire, police, and emergency services; maintain local roads; run municipal and regional public transportation systems; and manage parks and recreation facilities. Some local governments also own utility companies, such as power plants, internet services, water and sewage systems, waste management, and recycling facilities. Additionally, they manage their own debt by making interest and principal payments.

A complicating factor in local government finances is the mandates and requirements flowing down from state and federal governments. These often require local governments to allocate and spend funds on certain programs, leaving little or no discretion. These flow-down requirements can represent a significant portion of the local government's annual budget.

The descriptions of service and policy areas for each level of government are not exhaustive. However, they illustrate the breadth of responsibilities encountered by those in public administration when managing government affairs. These descriptions also help the reader understand that public administrators must deal the needs of a variety of constituencies. Each constituency group seeks to influence government decisions on a range of policy and operational issues (Rubin, 1998, p.29). The broad scope of responsibilities and the diversity of constituencies require public administrators to possess a working knowledge of public financial management to serve their jurisdictions in a professional, competent, and ethical manner.

Our purpose in describing the roles of various levels of government is to reinforce the importance of understanding public financial management. Individuals working as public administrators should be concerned with the effective, efficient, and economical use of financial resources available to meet the needs of the communities they serve and achieve the strategic and operational objectives of their governments. Virtually every decision they make will affect government finances, underscoring the need financial management knowledge and expertise.

Public financial management requires knowledge of several disciplines, including economics, finance, accounting, political science, and general business administration (Jordan & Hackbart, 2022, p.11). Effective public financial management systems are necessary to ensure government accountability for resource use, minimize waste, and maintain transparency in decision-making.

Next, we will examine the key aspects of financial management, with particular emphasis on budgeting. While most of our attention will focus on the federal system, we will also include state and local government.

OVERVIEW OF PUBLIC FINANCIAL MANAGEMENT

Public financial management for all U.S. governments is driven by law, whether through their respective constitution or charter, or through laws or ordinances passed by their legislative bodies and signed by the chief executive. Regardless of the level—federal, state, or local—the process generally follows similar lines. Governments must be able to pay their bills to function effectively.

Unlike private businesses, which are initially capitalized through contributions from owners, investors, and creditors and later maintain their operations through revenues from the sale of goods and services, governments raise funds primarily through taxes and fees levied on taxpayers.

The government financial management process typically begins with the creation, execution, and monitoring of a budget. As discussed in earlier chapters, modern public budgeting usually starts with individual units of government providing the executive branch with the necessary information to generate a budget proposal. This proposal is then sent to the legislative body for consideration and eventual passage. The budget that emerges from the legislative process is reviewed by the executive branch, were it may be signed, rejected, or passed through inaction. Once approved, the budget is monitored throughout the year to ensure compliance by those given permission to use the allocated funds.

Each government has a designated unit responsible for managing bill payments. As funds are committed and spent, transactions are usually run through this unit, which often conducts reviews or audits to ensure compliance with laws or ordinances governing expenditures. Similarly, governments typically have a unit responsible for collecting and managing funds owed by taxpayers and citizens who pay fees for certain government services.

At the end of each fiscal year, governments are required to prepare an annual comprehensive financial report (ACFR). Governments record all financial trans-actions in computerized accounting systems following generally accepted accounting principles (GAAP) as created and issued by the government accounting standards board (GASB). These reports are produced in accordance with respective laws the best practices published by the Government Finance Officers Association (GFOA). The annual cycle generally concludes with the performance and reporting of a financial audit performed in accordance with generally accepted auditing standards (GAAS), with results formally reported.

In the following sections, we will describe the federal process in more detail, followed by an overview of state and local processes. We want to remind readers that this is a brief introduction to public financial management, intended to provide a basic understanding and a foundation for further study. Our illustrations of state and local processes will focus on the state of Georgia and the city of Atlanta, Georgia.

OVERVIEW OF FEDERAL FINANCIAL MANAGEMENT

Before we explain the current federal financial management process, it may be helpful to briefly consider its historical context. For the first 130 years of the nation's history, public financial management was dominated by the Congress, as stipulated in the Constitution (Saturno, 2020, October 1; Saturno, 2023, January 10; Stiff, 2020, June 16). Congress authorized programs and agencies and appropriated funds, while the U.S. Treasury managed the nation's cash and paid its bills. In the federal system, no public official could spend money without Congress appropriating those funds. The budget process required to enact appropriation laws complex and highly decentralized, leaving the president largely on the sidelines watching as it unfolded. While Congress made various attempts to organize the process by restructuring its committee structure, it was not until 1921 that a significant legislative reorganization occurred (Dearborn, 2019).

In 1921, Congress passed and the president signed the Budget and Accounting Act, establishing a national budget system that, with modifications, persists to this day (Krause & Jin, 2020; Saturno, 2023, January 10). The Act introduced four major provisions: (1) it established a federal budget framework requiring the president to submit an annual budget for the entire federal government to the Congress; (2) it created the Bureau of the Budget (now the Office of Management and Budget) to help the president in managing budget responsibilities; (3) it established the General Accounting Office (now the Government Accountability Office) responsible for audits, evaluations, and investigations to report findings to Congress; and (4) it required an annual independent audit of the government's accounts.

Over fifty years later, Congress addressed further issues with the budgeting process through the Congressional Budget and Impoundment Control Act of 1974 (Saturno, 2023, January 10). This legislation reorganized Congress's budget responsibilities to create a more systematic process. The Act established budget committees in both the House and Senate and created the Congressional Budget

Office (CBO) to provide Congress with nonpartisan economic and budgetary analyses. It revised the budget process to better coordinate between the House and Senate in passing a budget, which now consists of twelve separate appropriations bills. Additionally, the Act gave Congress the ability to prevent the president from withholding appropriated funds without proper authorization and included a rule barring unrelated amendments from being added to budget reconciliation bills. While other legislation has affected the federal budgetary process, these two acts remain the most significant.

The U.S. federal government's budgeting process is a complex, multi-stage procedure involving various branches and agencies (Saturno, 2023, January 10). The process typically begins with the president submitting a budget proposal to Congress, outlining spending priorities and revenue estimates. Congress then reviews and debates the proposal through a system of appropriations committees and subcommittees before considering it as a full body in each chamber. The House of Representatives and the Senate must pass budget resolutions, which guide subsequent spending bills. Once both chambers agree on a budget, it goes to the president for approval. Disagreements between Congress and the president can lead to negotiations, and in some cases, government shutdowns can occur if a budget is not approved by the start of the fiscal year.

This process is designed to allocate funds for government operations, programs, and services while addressing economic priorities and fiscal responsibility.

Figure 9.1: Federal Budget Process Outline

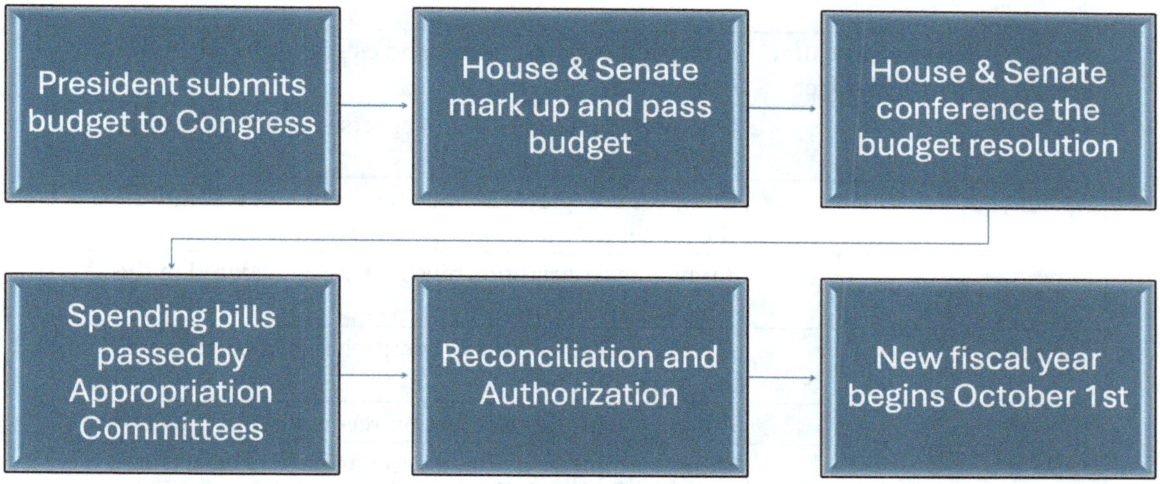

President submits budget to Congress	→	House & Senate mark up and pass budget	→	House & Senate conference the budget resolution
Spending bills passed by Appropriation Committees	→	Reconciliation and Authorization	→	New fiscal year begins October 1st

The Congressional Research Service (CRS) publishes detailed reports explaining the federal budgeting process (Congressional Research Services, 2012 July 27; Saturno, 2023, January 10; S.Prt. 117-23, 2022, December). The president's actual budget proposal sent to Congress can be found on the homepage of the Office of Management and Budget (OMB). Additional information about Congress' role in the budgeting process can is available through three key resources: the House Budgeting Committee,[1] the Senate Budgeting Committee,[2] and the Congressional Budget Office.[3] This brief overview of the budgeting process is based on information from these sources and the CRS reports.

The federal budget process is highly complex and often fraught with politics and conflict, which frequently prevents Congress from passing a final budget before the start of the new fiscal year, on October 1. According to a Pew Center article (Desilver, 2023, September 13), Congress successfully passed all required budgetary bills only four times since the Congressional Budgetary Act of 1974 (CBA) was enacted. These years were 1977, 1989, 1995, and 1997. In each of the other 45 years, at least one continuing resolution was required to keep the government operating.

Although the CBA was intended to bring structure and organization to the budget process, the reality is that it remains a "messy" process. It is often marked by frequent conflicts, threats of government shutdowns, and the need for continuing resolutions.

The legally-defined timetable for the annual budget process is outlined in the following table (Aherne, 2023, July 27; Congressional Research Services, 2023, March 20). The primary challenges in passing the budget usually arise during congressional committee and subcommittee meetings, as well as during full-body debates.

Table 9.1. Congressional Budget Process Timetable[4]

On or before:	Action to be completed:
First Monday in February	President submits a budget proposal to Congress.
February 15	Congressional Budget Office submits report to budget committees.
Not later than 6 weeks after president submits budget	Committees submit views and estimates to the budget committees.
April 1	Senate Budget Committee reports concurrent resolution on the budget.
April 15	Congress completes action on concurrent resolution on the budget.
May 15	Annual appropriations bills may be considered in the House.
June 10	House Appropriations Committee reports last annual appropriation bill.
June 15	Congress completes action on reconciliation legislation.
June 30	House completes action on reconciliation legislation.
October 1	Fiscal year begins.

---

1 https://budget.house.gov/

2 https://www.budget.senate.gov/

3 https://www.cbo.gov/

4 https://crsreports.congress.gov Report No. R46240

The president must have help in managing the budget preparation process. Congress, in formalizing the budget process in the early 20th century, passed the Budgeting and Accounting Act of 1921 (Library of Congress, n.d.). In this act, Congress created the Office of Management and Budget (OMB) to assist the president in carrying out the budget preparation and management process (Congressional Research Services, 2006, March 31). The OMB has three primary functions: (1) coordinating the preparation and submission of the president's budget, (2) managing the apportionment of funds after the enactment of the appropriations bills, and (3) tracking and reporting to the president on spending by agencies to ensure compliance with the budget and the related laws (Congressional Research Services, 2022, May 5). Each agency in the executive branch has its own budget function, responsible for preparing the individual budget request that is sent on to the president.

The framework currently used by Congress was formalized in 1974 with the passage of the Congressional Budget Act (CBA) (Saturno, 2023, January 10). The CBA requires Congress to adopt a budget resolution that sets overall spending and revenue levels for the federal government. Congress uses this resolution to organize its work on the annual budget. The CBA also created a budget committee in each house of the Congress and the Congressional Budget Office (CBO). The CBO is an independent agency that provides Congress with non-partisan analysis of economic and budgetary issues (Congressional Budget Office, n.d.). The CBO assists Congress with the development and evaluation of the budget resolution.

The CBA established a structure to help organize the work of the budget and define the various roles played by committees.[5] It reinforced the division between authorization and appropriations. Authorizing legislation focuses on programmatic issues, while appropriations deal with program finances. Congress currently operates twelve appropriation subcommittees that report to the House or Senate Appropriations Committee. These subcommittees work on budget issues related to specific policy areas. The CBA also created a budget committee in each of house of Congress. These committees are responsible for developing and overseeing the budget resolution and coordinating the budget process within and between the two houses. The budget committees also play a role in the reconciliation process because, often, the two houses adopt final budgets that do not agree.

STATE BUDGET PROCESS

All states have a budget process established by law. Much like the federal system, this process typically involve both the executive and legislative branches and results in the legal adoption of an annual budget to ensure state agencies can continue operating and managing the programs under their jurisdiction. In this section, we will briefly examine the state of Georgia's budget process (Georgia Budget and Policy Institute, n.d.). However, most states provide detailed information through

---

5   https://budget.house.gov/about/committee

the Governor's Office or the state legislature's committee pages explaining their specific budget processes.

The Office of Planning and Budget (OPB) explains the budget process in Georgia by dividing it into seven phases. We will summarize each phase below (Carl Vinson Institute of Government, n.d.).

The process begins with phase one, where the governor sends a memo to state agencies requesting that they prepare and submit their budget requests to the Office of Planning and Budget along with their strategic plan (Carl Vinson Institute of Government, n.d.). In both theory and practice, the budget reflects the agency's strategic plan expressed in monetary units, so the linkage between the two documents makes good sense. Georgia's budget process has three primary objectives: (1) improving services, (2) increasing employee retention, and (3) enhancing overall efficiency. The strategic plan and budget are expected to show how the agency plans to achieve these objectives.

The second phase occurs concurrently with the first and involves the governor setting the state's revenue estimate (Carl Vinson Institute of Government, n.d.). Consistent with sound business practices, the state has an estimate of available to allocate before reviewing all budget requests.

In the third phase, the Office of Planning and Budget analyzes the revenue estimate and budget requests and prepares recommendations for the governor's consideration. This phase ends with the governor drafting a formal budget recommendation for submission to the state legislature.

The fourth and fifth phases encompass the legislative process, which leads to the adoption of the state's formal budget (Carl Vinson Institute of Government, n.d.). First, the House of Representatives considers the governor's recommendations and develops an appropriations bill. This bill is broken down into line items for each agency and program. Once passed by the House, the bill is sent to the Senate for consideration and vote. If the House and Senate versions differ, a conference committee made up of members from both chambers meets to negotiate a final version. Once both chambers approve the final version, it moves to the governor for consideration.

In the fifth phase, the governor has forty days to sign the bill, or it automatically becomes law (Carl Vinson Institute of Government, n.d.). The governor may use a line-item veto to remove specific parts of the budget. Once the bill is signed into law, the OPB prepares the "Budget in Brief," a document summarizing the budget and noting any important highlights.

The sixth phase is the implementation phase. During this phase, the OPB works with individual agencies to ensure budgets are not exceeded. The OPB reviews and approves agency operating budgets, oversees monthly allotments, and monitors agency expenditures.

The seventh and final phase occurs at the end of the fiscal year when the state auditor conducts an audit of each agency's expenditures.

LOCAL GOVERNMENT BUDGET PROCESS

Local governments—including counties, cities, townships, special districts, and school districts (Census of Government, 2017)—follow a similar budget process. General information about municipal (city) governments' budgets can often be found on the website of each state's municipal association. For example, the Georgia Municipal Association (GMA) provides resources related to municipal budgets, and a link to the GMA is included in the references section of this chapter.

To illustrate, we located a description of the budget process for Atlanta, Georgia. Similar to the state budget process, the mayor requests city departments to prepare and submit individual budgets, which are then consolidated into a formal executive budget request. This request is submitted to the city council for consideration. The city council holds public hearings and is required to adopt a budget by June, prior to the start of the new fiscal year.

The City of Atlanta also has a budget commission that develops a revenue estimate for the upcoming fiscal year (City of Atlanta, n.d.). This information, along with recommendations from the city council, is made available to the mayor and chief financial officer to consider in drafting their budget proposal. Once the budget is adopted, city departments work with the Office of Budget and Fiscal Policy within the finance department to implement and manage their individual budgets. This office also assists city departments in preparing their annual budget requests.

The governmental budget process is of paramount importance, as it serves as the fiscal blueprint guiding the allocation of public resources while ensuring transparency, accountability, and effective governance. Unlike private sector budgets, government budgets encompass a diverse array of public services and programs aimed at meeting the needs and priorities of a broad and varied citizenry.

Government budgets play a critical role in shaping public policy, addressing societal challenges, and fostering economic stability. The process involves intricate negotiations, public input, and approval by governing bodies, reflecting the democratic principles underpinning the allocation of taxpayer funds. In contrast to private sector budgets, which primarily focus on profit and shareholder value, government budgets emphasize the provision of public goods and services, such as education, healthcare, infrastructure, and defense.

The challenge lies in balancing fiscal responsibility with the evolving demands of a dynamic society, making the governmental budget process an intricate and crucial aspect of democratic governance.

FINANCIAL ACCOUNTING, REPORTING, ANALYSIS, AND CONTROLS

This final section of the chapter revisits some material mentioned earlier and introduces some new material. We wanted to emphasize its relative importance without it getting lost in the details of the budget process. Here, we will briefly address financial accounting, financial reporting, financial analysis, and internal controls.

Financial accounting in government involves systematically recording, analyzing, and reporting financial transactions to provide accurate and transparent information about the government's financial position and performance. Governmental accounting follows specific principles and standards set by accounting bodies such as the Governmental Accounting Standards Board (GASB) in the United States (www.gasb.org). This includes preparing financial statements, such as the Statement of Net Position and the Statement of Activities, which convey the government's fiscal health and operational results.

Government accounting differs from private-sector accounting in several unique ways. While the government produces two government-wide statements resembling the accrual statements of private businesses, it also uses fund accounting to track current resources allocated for specific purposes, such as special revenue funds or capital projects funds. Fund accounting is based on a modified accrual basis, as opposed to a full accrual basis, to facilitate the reporting of only current financial information in the fund financial statements. Additionally, budgetary accounting plays a central role, focusing on comparing actual financial results with budgeted amounts to ensure fiscal responsibility and accountability—an emphasis unique to government financial reporting.

Financial reporting in government goes beyond merely preparing financial statements. It includes the creation of the Annual Comprehensive Financial Report (ACFR), which provides a detailed overview of the government's financial condition. The ACFR contains financial statements, management discussions and analyses, statistical information, and supplemental details. Transparency and accountability are key goals of financial reporting, enabling citizens, investors, and other stakeholders to assess how public funds are managed and used for the community's benefit. Most U.S. governments follow the guidelines and best practices published by the Government Finance Officers Association (www.gfoa.org).

Financial analysis in government interprets the financial data to evaluate efficiency, effectiveness, and sustainability of government operations (ICMA, 2019; McDonald, 2017). Analysts may assess trends, ratios, and key performance indicators to gain insights into the financial health of a government entity. Comparative analysis between budgeted and actual figures helps identify variances, facilitating informed decision-making. Financial analysis is a crucial tool for policymakers and government officials to make strategic decisions, allocate resources effectively, and ensure responsible fiscal management.

Internal controls are an essential part of any financial accounting and reporting system. In government, internal controls are mechanisms designed to safeguard assets, ensure the accuracy of financial reporting, and promote compliance with laws and regulations (www.coso.org). The Government Accountability Office (GAO) also publishes the *Green Book*, which outlines important internal controls for government operations. Internal controls encompass a range of activities, including segregation of duties, authorization processes, and physical safeguards. Regular audits and reviews assess the effectiveness of these internal controls.

Effective internal controls help prevent fraud, errors, and the mismanagement of public funds, contributing to the reliability and integrity of financial information in government financial statements.

Advancements in technology play a significant role in enhancing financial accounting, reporting, analysis, and internal controls in government. Integrated financial management systems streamline processes, improve data accuracy, and enable real-time reporting. However, governments also face challenges, particularly the need for cybersecurity measures to protect sensitive financial information.

Balancing the benefits of technology with its associated risks requires ongoing vigilance to ensure the reliability, security, and efficiency of financial processes. This is especially critical in the ever-evolving landscape of governmental finance.

REFERENCES

Aherne, D. C. (2023, July 27). *The congressional budget process timeline.* (CRS Report No. R47235). https://crsreports.congress.gov/product/pdf/R/R47235

Appleby, P. H. (1947). Harold D. Smith—Public administrator. *Public Administration Review, 7*(2), 77–81. https://doi.org/10.2307/972748

Carl Vinson Institute of Government. (n.d.). *Typical state budget process in Georgia.* Retrieved February 14, 2024, from https://cviog.uga.edu/_resources/documents/publications/handbook-galeg-budget.pdf

Census of Government. (2017). *Local governments by type and by state (Table 2).* Retrieved February 23, 2024, https://www.census.gov/data/tables/2017/econ/gus/2017-governments.html

City of Atlanta, Georgia. (n.d.). *Office of budget and fiscal policy.* Retrieved February 14, 2024, from https://www.atlantaga.gov/government/departments/finance/budget-fiscal-policy

Congressional Budget Office. (n.d.). Retrieved from https://www.cbo.gov/

Congressional Research Services. (2006, March 31). *Office of management and budget (OMB): A brief overview.* (CRS Report No. RS21665). https://crsreports.congress.gov/product/pdf/RS/RS21665

Congressional Research Services. (2012, July 27). *The executive budget process: An overview.* (CRS Report No. R42633). https://crsreports.congress.gov/product/pdf/R/R42633

Congressional Research Services. (2022, May 5). *The role of the office of management and budget (OMB) in budget development: In brief.* (CRS Report No. R47089). https://crsreports.congress.gov/product/pdf/R/R47089

Congressional Research Services. (2023, March 20). *The executive budget process timeline: In brief.* (CRS Report No. R47088). https://crsreports/congress.gov/product/pdf/R/R47088

Dearborn, J. A. (2019). The "proper organs" for presidential representation: A fresh look at the budget and accounting act of 1921. *Journal of Policy History. 31*(1), 1–41. https://doi.org/10.1017/S0898030618000325

Desilver, D. (2023, September 13). Congress has long struggled to pass spending bills on time. *Pew research center*, retrieved February 23, 2024, https://www.pewresearch.org/short-reads/2023/09/13/congress-has-long-struggled-to-pass-spending-bills-on-time

Gabrini, C. J. (2022). Auditing and internal controls. In B. D. McDonald & M. M. Meagan (Eds.), *Teaching public budgeting and finance: A practical guide* (pp. 155–170). Routledge Public Affairs Education. https://doi.org/10.4324/9781003240440

Georgia Budget and Policy Institute. (n.d.). *Overview of Georgia's 2025 fiscal year budget*. Retrieved February 14, 2024, from https://gbpi.org/overview-of-georgias-2025-fiscal-year-budget/

Georgia Municipal Association. (n.d.). *A budget guide for Georgia's municipalities*. Retrieved February 14, 2024, from https://www.gacities.com/Resources/GMA-Handbooks-Publications/A-Budget-Guide-for-Georgias-Municipalities.aspx

Georgia Public Policy Foundation. (n.d.). *Fiscal overview*. Retrieved February 14, 2024, from, https://www.georgiapolicy.org/publications/2020-guide-to-the-issues/fiscal-overview/

Government Accounting Standards Board (GASB). (n.d.). Retrieved from https://www.gasb.org/

Government Finance Officers Association (GFOA). (n.d.). *Budgeting best practices*. Retrieved February 14, 2024, from https://www.gfoa.org/best-practices/budgeting

Governor's Office of Planning and Budget. (n.d.). *The budget process*. State of Georgia. Retrieved February 14, 2024, from https://opb.georgia.gov/budget-information/budget-process

Governor's Office of Planning and Budget. (n.d.). *Budget documents*. State of Georgia. Retrieved February 14, 2024, from https://opb.georgia.gov/budget-information/budget-documents

ICMA. (2019). *Getting started: Performance management for local government*, (2nd ed.). International City/County Management Association.

Internal Revenue Service. (n.d.). Retrieved from https://www.irs.gov/about-irs

Johnson, C. L., & Abbas, Y. (2022). Financial management. In B. D. McDonald & M. M. Meagan (Eds.), *Teaching public budgeting and finance: A practical guide* (pp. 109–154). Routledge Public Affairs Education. https://doi.org/10.4324/9781003240440

Jordan, M. M. & Hackbart, M. (2022). Public budgeting and finance in context. In B. D. McDonald & M. M. Meagan (Eds.), *Teaching public budgeting and finance: A practical guide* (pp. 9–29). Routledge Public Affairs Education. https://doi.org/10.4324/9781003240440

Krause, G. A. & Jin, R. Q. (2020). Organizational design and its consequences for administrative reform: Historical lessons from the U.S. Budget and Accounting Act of

1921. *Governance, 33*, 365–384. https://doi.org/10.1111/gove.12435

Library of Congress. (n.d.). *Research guide, federal Budget: Sources of information, understanding the past*. Retrieved from https://guides.loc.gov/federal-budget/past-understanding

McDonald, B. III. (2017). *Measuring the fiscal health of municipalities*. (Working Paper WP17BM1.) Lincoln Institute of Land Policy.

Miller, G. J. (1991). *Government financial management theory*. Marcel Dekker, Inc.

Ross, J. M., & Duncan, D. R. (2022). Revenue. In B. D. McDonald & M. M. Meagan (Eds.), *Teaching public budgeting and finance: A practical guide* (pp. 30–50). Routledge Public Affairs Education. https://doi.org/10.4324/9781003240440

Rubin, I. S. (1998). *Class, tax, & power: Municipal budgeting in the United States*. Chatham House Publishers, Inc.

Saturno, J. V. (2020, October 1). *The origination clause of the U.S. Constitution: Interpretation and enforcement*. (CRS Report No. R46558). https://crsreports/congress.gov/product/pdf/R/R46558

Saturno, J. V. (2023, January 10). *Introduction to the federal budget process*. (CRS Report No. R46240). https://crsreports.congress.gov/product/pdf/R/R46240

Smith, H. D. (1944). The budget as an instrument of Legislative Control and Executive Management. *Public Administration Review, 4*(3), 181–188. https://doi.org/10.2307/972547

S. Prt. 117-23. (2022, December). *The congressional budget process*. Retrieved from https://www.congress.gov/senate-prints/117th-congress

Stiff, S. M. (2020, June 16). *Congress's power over appropriations: Constitutional and statutory provisions*. (CRS Report No. R46417). https://crsreports.congress.gov/product/pdf/R/R46417

The White House. (n.d.). *The Office of Management and Budget*. Retrieved from https://www.whitehouse.gov/omb/

United States House of Representatives. (n.d.). *House Budget Committee*. Retrieved from https://budget.house.gov/

United States Senate. (n.d.). *Senate Budget Committee*. Retrieved from https://www.budget.senate.gov/

United States Treasury. (n.d.). *How much has the government spent this year?* Retrieved from https://fiscaldata.treasury.gov/americas-finance-guide/federal-spending/

Urban Institute. (n.d.). *State and local backgrounders*. Retrieved from https://www.urban.org/policy-centers/cross-center-initiatives/state-and-local-finance-initiative/state-and-local-backgrounders/state-and-local-expenditures

USAID. (n.d.). *Public financial management*. Retrieved February 25, 2024, from https://www.fpfinancingroadmap.org/learning/specific-topics/public-financial-management

Willoughby, K. G. & Jensen, C. (2022). Public budgeting mechanics. In B. D.

McDonald & M. M. Meagan (Eds.), *Teaching public budgeting and finance: A practical guide* (pp. 51–74). Routledge Public Affairs Education. https://doi.org/10.4324/9781003240440

McDonald & M. M. Meagan (Eds.), *Teaching public budgeting and finance: A practical guide* (pp. 51–74). Routledge Public Affairs Education. https://doi.
org/10.4324/9781003240440

10 Reflections on Public Administration: Key Takeaways and Challenges

LEARNING OBJECTIVES

Students completing this chapter should be able to:

1. Summarize the key takeaways from chapters one through nine.
2. Explain the challenges in leading and managing public organizations.
3. Discuss challenges involving conflict in society and politics.
4. Discuss challenges involving the global nature of business and politics.
5. Discuss challenges involving technology and innovation.

INTRODUCTION

In writing this textbook, we aimed to share with students our understanding of the major issues facing public administrators. Not everyone who studies public administration or reads this book will work in government or seek government employment. Our audience likely includes many who will work in other settings but will interact with those serving as public administrators. We hope that the material in this textbook will help students and readers appreciate government and those who choose to serve the public.

This chapter is the final chapter in this book, but it is not the end of the story. Any one of the issues or topics we covered here could be the focus of an entire course. In this chapter, we will briefly summarize the main topics and issues addressed throughout the book. This will be followed by a section on the key similarities and differences between managing private businesses and government. Finally, we will share our thoughts on the current and future challenges facing public administration.

SUMMARY OF MAIN TOPICS

In the previous nine chapters, students were introduced to various topics important to understanding the nature and scope of public administration (chapter one). While not intended to be comprehensive, the goal in this text is to help students develop an appreciation for the public sector environment and provide a foundation for further study. We explored how the foundation of public administration in the United States is rooted in the Constitution (chapter two). The U.S. is a nation governed by laws, and it is through these laws that the administrative structure has evolved since the nation's founding.

Over time, different frameworks have been proposed to explain the purpose and function of public administration in the United States (chapter three). These paradigms help frame the study of public administration and clarify why our system looks as it does today.

There are fundamental differences between the private and public sectors. While both are concerned with the effective, efficient, and economical use of resources (human, physical, and financial capital) to achieve established goals and objectives, there are key differences in their specific goals, objectives, and decision-making processes (chapters four, five, and eight). The private sector is primarily focused on creating value, as measured through financial performance (e.g., profit and earnings per share), financial position (e.g., various financial ratios), and an investor's definition of value (typically ownership share value).

The public sector also acknowledges the importance of financial management (chapter nine); however, its primary focus lies elsewhere. Government and not-for-profit organizations typically prioritize allocating resources and services to stakeholders or constituents, including individual citizens, families, or other organizations. Values such as fairness and equity often guide the goals and objectives of public sector programs. Public sector organizations in the United States owe their existence to the rule of law and the Constitutional system of government. Decisions are made through a complex legislative and regulatory process that many citizens find difficult to follow and appreciate. The term "red tape" is often used to describe the resulting structure of laws, rules, and regulations.

Nothing happens in government without the work of those who serve in federal, state, and local government (chapter six). Over U.S. history, public sector employment has shifted from being dominated by wealthy landowners to a patronage system supporting elected officials. However, abuses within the patronage system led to the emergence of a more structured and regulated civil service. This civil service system, designed to protect the integrity of the administrative process, continues to evolve and strengthen to this day (chapter seven).

This final chapter addresses several pressing issues and challenges that impact current decision-making and will continue to do so in the future. These challenges include the ongoing pressure to administer government more like a private business, based on the assumption that private sector practices can be easily transferred to the public sphere. Other challenges derive from societal and political conflicts, including racism, immigration, social unrest involving law enforcement and the military, global competition and conflict, and the rapid growth of artificial intelligence and its integration into all technologies.

Finally, we offer a few concluding thoughts for students to consider as they wrap up their study of public administration. It is our hope that students will continue their studies beyond this course and text.

MANAGING AND LEADING PUBLIC ORGANIZATIONS

A recurring debate in politics has been whether the government can be run more like a private business (Hood, 1995; Allison, 1980; Weinberg 1983). This topic was not address in depth in any of the earlier chapters, as we saved it for this concluding chapter. The motivation behind this debate stems from a desire to simplify and streamline government operations, making them more responsive to citizens and more accountable for the financial resources raised through compulsory taxes and fees. In this section, we will briefly summarize the history of this debate, describe the similarities and differences between government and private business, and review past presidential administrations' efforts to reorganize government to enhance operational efficiency and effectiveness.

The debate about running the government more like a business is not new. In fact, it dates back to the late 19th century with the work of Frederick Taylor and the methods of scientific management (see chapter eight). Taylor's methods focused on finding the most efficient ways to accomplish tasks while minimizing fatigue. In 1912, Taylor testified before Congress, advocating for the application of scientific management principles to public organizations (Taylor Society, 1926). He specifically recommended adopting more systematic methods of management, redesigning tasks into logical, easily definable and measurable steps, improving worker selection and training, and obtaining worker buy-in to successfully implement these new methods.

During the early 20th century, the United States experienced the rise of the Progressive Era of government (see chapter two). This movement sought to enhance the efficiency and effectiveness of government agencies while increasing their responsiveness to satisfying citizens' needs. This period from the 1880s to the 1920s brought significant reforms, including the establishment of the civil service system, increased regulation of private businesses, and a focus on reducing corruption in both government and business. As noted in chapter two, several independent regulatory agencies were also created during this time.

Fast forward to the 1980s and 1990s, the New Public Management (NPM) movement emerged (Hood, 1995). During this era, political leaders and academics promoted the adoption of private-sector management techniques within public-sector organizations. These practices included performance measurement, decentralization, competition, and outsourcing. There was also an increased emphasis on privatizing certain government services that paralleled those already provided by the private sector.

This led to intense discussion and debate about the appropriateness of operating government more like a business (Osborne & Gaebler, 1992). While there are similarities between managing a government organization and a private business, there are important differences. Both settings rely on the same basic management functions, including planning, organizing, leading, and controlling resources to achieve established goals. Effective communication, decision-making, and problem-solving skills are essential in any organization. Additionally, both government and private-sector businesses rely on fostering a positive work environment to motivate employees, as well as on employee performance and retention.

However, there are significant differences between managing government and business (see chapters eight and nine). The primary goal of a business is to earn a profit, whereas government agencies serve the public good and focus on achieving specific program mandates. Private business offers managers a greater degree of flexibility in decision-making, while managers in government operate following complex procedures that often require multiple layers of approval. Business management focuses on selling products and services in competitive markets, whereas government raises revenue through compulsory taxes and agencies rely on a complex budget process to secure appropriated funds. Performance in private businesses is typically measured through financial metrics focused on profitability, while government performance is assessed based on service delivery, societal impact, and compliance with rules and regulations. Furthermore, businesses are primarily accountable to stockholders, while the government is accountable to a wide range of constituencies, including citizens, elected officials, and oversight bodies.

Throughout this textbook, we have referred to "bureaucracy." According to Shafritz (2004), bureaucracy refers to the "totality of government offices or bureaus that constitute the permanent government of a state; that is, those public functions that continue regardless of changes in political leadership" (p.34). By the 1980s, "bureaucracy" seemed a derogatory word, often associated with "red tape" (Kaufman, 1977). Red tape refers to what people consider the excessive formality of policies and procedures required to accomplish tasks. Another term, "reorganization," refers to changes in administrative structures and formal procedures intended to make government more efficient and effective. In this final chapter, we want to close the loop of the bureaucracy discussion by addressing a few of the major reorganization efforts undertaken by U.S. presidents to improve government operations.

Several presidents are remembered for their signature efforts to reorganize the federal government (Ingraham, 1995). The first was President Thomas Jefferson, who served as the third president of the United States from 1801 to 1809. Jefferson's presidency was marked by efforts to strengthen the executive while reforming the federal government to reduce its influence on society. His efforts focused on limiting the federal government and giving more sovereignty to states. While other presidents have also sought to affect the size and scope of the federal government, we now shift our focus from the nation's early years to the first half of the 20th century to examine other administrations and the confounding factors they faced.

On October 29, 1929, the United States suffered experienced the stock market crash, an event now known as "Black Tuesday." The economic fallout from the crisis led to the election of Franklin Delano Roosevelt (FDR) as president. Serving from 1933 to 1945, FDR worked with Congress to address the economic depression by passing a series of laws collectively known as the New Deal. This legislation marked a significant expansion of the federal government's role (Lee, 1982).

The New Deal had three primary objectives: economic recovery, poverty relief, and financial system reform. At least seven federal agencies established during the New Deal era remain in operation today. (See Table 10.1 for details.)

Table 10.1: Currently Operating Federal Agencies from New Deal Era[1]

Year	Agency Title (current)	Abbreviation
1935	Social Security Administration	SSA
1934	Securities and Exchange Commission	SEC
1934	Federal Housing Authority	FHA
1934	Federal Communications Commission	FCC
1933	Federal Deposit Insurance Corporation	FDIC
1933	Farm Credit Agency	FCA
1933	Tennessee Valley Authority	TVA

Following World War II, President Harry S. Truman worked with Congress and the military to address the new challenges facing the nation and the world. The result of these efforts was the passage of the National Security Act of 1947 (Nelson, 1985). The Act centralized the military by creating the Department of Defense to replace the former Department of War. It also formalized the nation's foreign policy by creating the Central Intelligence Agency (CIA) and The National Security Council (NSC) to address Cold War challenges in the post-WWII environment (Rearden, 1984).

Although 100 years had passed since the Civil War was fought over the practice of slavery, the 1960s were still marked by widespread discrimination and racism. Lyndon B. Johnson, initially vice president under John F. Kennedy, assumed the presidency after JFK's assassination. Johnson's administration was marked by a series of legislative actions known as the Great Society (Shafritz, 2004, p 139). This legislation focused on addressing racial injustice, poverty, and other social issues, such as housing, leading to the creation of the Department of Housing and Urban Development. During Johnson's presidency, the Social Security program was expanded to include Medicare for older adults and Medicaid for economically-disadvantaged individuals.[2]

---

1 Lee, 1982

2 https://ssa.gov/history

Following a decade of political scandals, economic hardship, and foreign policy challenges (e.g., the Iran Hostage Crisis), Ronald Reagan, a former Democratic governor of California, was elected president as a Republican in 1980. Reagan's presidency emphasized privatizing government services through the authority granted in the Office of Management and Budget (OMB) Circular A-76 (Luckey, 2003). The 1980s also saw a period of deregulation across industries such as telecommunications and transportation.

Lastly, we examine the presidential administration of William J. Clinton (1992–2000). The government reforms during the 1990s significantly shaped public administration theory and practice, effects that continue to the present day. These reforms focused on reorganizing how government does business to make them more effective and efficient. A hallmark of this reform movement, referred to as New Public Management, was the emphasis on performance measurement.

This section has only briefly touched on many of the topics mentioned. Students are encouraged to explore these periods in American history further through additional reading, most of which is freely available online.

CHALLENGES: CONFLICT IN SOCIETY AND POLITICS

According to a Pew study (2021) examining societal conflict, the United States ranks first in societal conflict because of divisions between political parties and racial disparities (Connaughton, 2021). The study also revealed that people in the U.S. not only disagreed on policy issues but also experienced a high level of disagreement over facts (Silver et al., 2021). These findings are not surprising. Two significant conflicts in the U.S. typify these results: the Black Lives Matter (BLM) social movement and the insurrection at the U.S. Capitol Building on January 6, 2021. Both conflicts spilled over into politics as well.

The Black Lives Matter movement emerged in response to high-profile incidents involving local law enforcement and black citizens, many of which resulted in the injury or death of black individuals. While not an exhaustive list, students can read in the news archives about Eric Garner, Michael Brown, Laquan McDonald, Tamir Rice, Walter Scott, Freddie Gray, Philando Castile, Justine Damond, Jordan Edwards, and Breonna Taylor, all of whom were killed during interactions with law enforcement.[3] While detailing all such cases is beyond the scope of this chapter, these incidents have led to calls for law enforcement reform across the United States, including calls to defund police departments. Increasingly, these incidents resulted in public outrage and widespread protests.

After the 2020 election, in which President Donald Trump lost to President Joseph Biden, enthusiastic followers of President Trump, reacting to speeches of Trump and his supporters, stormed the U.S. Capitol Building. This attack caused extensive damage to the facility; led to the injury and death of several individuals,

---

3   AP A look at high-profile cases over killings by U.S. police (2021).

including local law enforcement; and forced the evacuation of our elected legislative leaders and their staff to secure their safety during the insurrection.[4] While the insurrection was ultimately put down, it demonstrated the anger and hatred some Americans feel toward those with differing political beliefs and policy positions on specific issues. Rather than discussing these differences and working out a compromise, the current political environment reflects a "winner-take-all" mentality and a "win-at-all costs" strategy.

This same level of conflict is affecting the use of impeachment as a political weapon instead of a governance tool (Cole & Garvey, 2023). According to usa.gov[5], there have been over sixty attempts to impeach federal officials. Most have been federal judges. Only twenty-one times have impeachments been successful and only eight times has it resulted in removal of an official from office. All eight were federal judges. Three presidents have been impeached: Andrew Johnson in 1868, Bill Clinton in 1998, and Donald Trump in 2019 and 2021. Attempts against Presidents John Tyler and James Buchanan were not successful, and President Richard Nixon resigned before he could be impeached. There was an unsuccessful attempt to impeach Vice President John Calhoun. The nation has seen six attempts to impeach cabinet secretaries; four were unsuccessful, two resigned before anything could happen, and two were successfully impeached.

The threat of impeachment has always existed and been used, but more recently, it seems the specter of impeachment comes up in every presidential term since President Clinton was impeached in 1998. In addition, the impeachment of Secretary of Homeland Security Alejandro Mayorkas in 2024 was the first since Secretary of War William Belknap in 1876. Some argue that the use of impeachment is a political weapon. It may well be true. Since Joseph Biden took office as president, republican legislators have continuously argued for impeachment hearings to investigate any involvement or knowledge the president may have had in his son's business dealings. The question for academics and practitioners is whether the divisions we see in society are being played out in politics.

CHALLENGES: GLOBAL NATURE OF BUSINESS AND POLITICS

An overview of public administration is not complete without considering the global nature of the subject matter. Shafritz's (2004) dictionary includes references to two key terms that caught this author's attention: globalism and global village (p. 132). He defines globalism as "a term describing U.S. foreign policy of active political and military involvement in all parts of the world; opposite of isolationism." He defines global village as "the notion that because of modern electronic communications, the people of the whole world have become as closely linked as the people in a premodern archetypal village." He also

---

4   https://www.gao.gov/blog/our-work-january-6th-attack

5   https://www.usa.gov/impeachment

references Marshall McLuhan's (1962) book *The Gutenberg Galaxy*, crediting it with coining the term.

McLuhan argues that technological innovation results—particularly in communication, starting with the printing press—have profoundly influenced culture and human consciousness. He writes, "but today, as electricity creates conditions of extreme interdependence on a global scale, we move swiftly again into an auditory world of simultaneous events and over-all awareness" (pp. 28–29). Later, he states, "but certainly, the electro-magnetic discoveries have recreated the simultaneous field in all human affairs so that the human family now exists under conditions of a global village. We live in a single constricted space resonant with tribal drums" (p. 31). He concludes, "the new electronic interdependence recreates the world in the image of a global village" (p. 31).

The global nature of public administration is not a new concept (Datar, 2006). Woodrow Wilson, often considered one of the first U.S. public administration scholars (Fukuyama, 2024), discussed the global nature of public administration in his 1887 article, "The Study of Administration." In this article, Wilson discussed the influence of British, French, and German experiences on the science of administration. The development of public administration in the United States did not occur in a vacuum but was influenced heavily by the experiences of other nations.

In chapter one of this book, we undertook defining public administration. It is once again useful to consider the definition of relevant terms. Merriam-Webster defines globalism as "a national policy of treating the whole world as a proper sphere for political influence." Globalization is defined as "the state of being globalized," with an example given of a globally-integrated economy. Students who have taken world history should recall that history is filled with episodes of nations acting on political, economic, and social global interests.

What has changed to increase our interest in or awareness of the global nature of public administration? According to Datar (2006), it is the "speed and extent of globalization" that has evolved. Innovations in transportation and communication technology have increased the speed and extent of globalization of all nation-states. Keohane and Nye (2000) define globalism as "a state of the world involving networks and interdependencies at multicontinental distances." They distinguish between the terms globalism, globalization, and interdependency.

Keohane and Nye (2000) define interdependency as "situations characterized by reciprocal effects among countries or among actors in different countries." They consider globalism to be a type of interdependency. To them, globalization refers to the degree of increase in globalism as opposed to isolationism. They further define globalism as multi-dimensional, identifying four specific dimensions: economic, military, environmental, and social or cultural globalism. While they admit that these categories are somewhat arbitrary, they serve to clarify the concept and its application. Economic globalism refers to the "long-distance flow of goods, services, and capital as well as the information and perceptions that accompany market exchange." Military globalism pertains to the use or threat of force worldwide. Environmental globalism involves "long-distance transport materials in the atmosphere, or oceans," including biological substances that "affect human health and well-being." Social or cultural globalism involves the spread of "ideas, information, images, and people" around the world.

When we consider the terms globalism and globalization, coupled with the rapid acceleration of technological innovation, we can begin to see how these factors impact public administration. Recently, the world has dealt with global financial crises, a global pandemic (COVID-19), immigration issues, and military conflicts in the Ukraine, Israel, and Iraq. Today's public administrators must do more than merely steering the course of their departments or agencies; they must also comprehend and respond to global influences and events that impact their policy arenas or geographic spheres of influence.

The global nature of public administration is apparent even at the local level of government. For example, the City of Chattanooga, Tennessee, maintains relationships with Wuxi, China; Hamm and Wolfsburg, Germany; Givatayim, Israel; Ganneung, Korea; Nizhnii Tagil, Russia; Tono, Japan; and Accra, Ghana. According to the Chattanooga government website, these relationships enrich the community, expand the economy, and broaden cultural horizons—touching on the dimensions of globalism described by Keohane and Nye.

Because the course associated with this textbook serves as an introduction to public administration, we encourage the serious student to study the subject beyond this course and beyond school. There is a renewed interest in comparative public administration (Haque, van der Wal, and van den Berg, 2021) and a growing recognition of its importance in public administration curricula (Leight & Abbott, 2022). Given the multidisciplinary nature of public administration, students would be well served by a strong knowledge base in economics, sociology, political science, management, and even the sciences and engineering (Farrell et al., 2022).

The next section of this chapter will explore technological innovation and its ongoing impact on public administration.

CHALLENGES: TECHNOLOGY AND INNOVATION

An entire chapter could have been devoted to the topic of technological innovation and its impact on public administration. However, space and time are limited, but we did not want to leave this discussion out of the book entirely. In chapter one, we explored the use of ChatGPT to begin our discussion of the differences between public and private organizations. We circle back to this example as we close out our textbook in this concluding chapter. Managing technological innovation is not a new challenge for public administrators. In 1945, the world changed with the use of two atomic weapons against Japan to end World War II. The effort required to develop these weapons was monumental. Considering that no infrastructure existed for a project of this type before the war, the president and his advisors had to start from scratch to engineer this technological feat.

There is a saying that necessity is the mother of invention, and nowhere has that been truer than in war. According to the Atomic Heritage Foundation,[6] President Roosevelt, under advice from notable scientists such as Albert Einstein, initiated the steps that led to the Manhattan Project, through which the U.S. nuclear program would be conducted. While no formal structure existed for managing technological innovation at the time, the efforts moved forward. Although President Roosevelt's administration oversaw the development of the nuclear program, it was ultimately President Truman's decision to deploy the new weapon in the Pacific theater.

Twelve years later, under President Eisenhower, a new threat emerged, resulting in the creation of the U.S. space program. In 1957, the Soviet Union launched the first satellite into orbit, causing grave concerns about how far behind the U.S. had fallen in the race to space.[7] Congress passed, and the president signed, a bill creating the National Aeronautics and Space Administration (NASA). Over the next twelve years, spanning three presidencies, the U.S. developed its own space program, culminating in the successful launch of a manned space mission to the moon.[8] Nothing captured the public's imagination more than a successful moon landing and safe return. This milestone occurred in the summer of 1969. In a span of under thirty years, citizens witnessed the birth of both the nuclear and space ages. But this is not the end of the story of technological innovation. Rather, it is the beginning of a story that continues to this day (see the following website: U.S. Space Force: https://www.spaceforce.mil/About-Us/About-Space-Force/History/).

To provide more structure around the management of technological innovation, President Gerald Ford initiated legislation that he later signed into law, creating the Office of Science and Technology Policy (OSTP). Upon signing the bill, President Ford quoted Thomas Jefferson: "knowledge is power; knowledge is safety, knowledge is happiness."[9] This new office would function within the Executive Office of the President (EOP) and "service as a source of scientific and technological analysis and judgment for the president with respect to major policies, plans, and programs of the federal government" (CRS, 2020, March 3). Since its creation in 1976, the OSTP has provided a structured approach for subsequent presidents to manage their policies related to the technological innovation.

Based on historical images of the OSTP website pages for Presidents Bush (2000-2008) and Obama (2009-2017), we learn about each president's concerns related to technology and innovation. President Bush's policy agenda focused on three main areas: cleaner and secure energy, transforming healthcare through information technology, and expanding broadband technology. President Obama's agenda included similar items: expanding broadband, advancing Healthcare IT,

---

6   Atomic Heritage Foundation History of the Manhattan Project

7   https://www.history.com/topics/cold-war/space-race

8   https://www.nasa.gov/history/

9   https://www.presidency.ucsb.edu/documents/remarks-upon-signing-the-national-science-and-technology-policy-organization-and

modernizing public safety communication systems, improving education through technology, clean energy development, and new manufacturing technologies.

The current OSTP website for President Biden focuses on artificial intelligence (AI). While other issues are important, recent developments have pushed AI to the forefront of any discussion on technology and innovation. In October 2023, President Biden issued Executive Order 14110, titled *Safe, Secure, and Trustworthy Development and Use of Artificial Intelligence*. The strategic objectives of this order center on determining how to effectively use AI in the private and public sectors while securing privacy and mitigating other risks associated with its development and use.

While the discussion so far has focused on the federal government, state governments are also interested in innovation and technology. For convenience—and because the authors are from Georgia—we focus on the state of Georgia. In 2000, the state legislature created the Georgia Technology Authority (GTA) (O.C.G.A. 50-24-7.10) and charged it with submitting an annual report compiling information from state agencies about their information technology spending. The mission of the GTA is to "provide technology leadership to the state of Georgia for sound IT enterprise management." Its program scope includes cybersecurity, artificial intelligence, broadband, constituent services, digital services, enterprise governance and planning, enterprise portfolio management, and technology innovation showcases.

The concerns and challenges associated with artificial intelligence are just beginning. Educators across the country are expressing concerns about its use and the risks of students relying on AI to violate academic honor codes. The challenge facing everyone is managing the temptation to abuse this new technology rather than embracing it to increase efficiency and effectiveness. Much like the computer and the software developed for it, AI is a tool with no inherent evil intent behind it. Any harm resulting from its use will be the responsibility of those choosing to use it in harmful ways, rather than enjoying its benefits.

CONCLUDING THOUGHTS

The end of this book is by no means the end of the story. Public administration is a dynamic field of study that will continually challenge those who wish to further their knowledge by reading and learning more about it. As we wrap up our coverage of this material, we hope students have learned that managing and leading in the public sector, while having some overlap with the private sector, presents a unique set of challenges.

While general principles of management and leadership often have opportunities to be transferred across sectors, they must be adapted to work effectively in the public sector. We wish readers well as they continue their education and hope that their study of public administration will help make them more informed leaders, managers, and citizens.

REFERENCES

Allison, G. T. (1980). Public and private management: are they fundamentally alike in all unimportant respects? (pp. 283–298). Cambridge, MA: Harvard University.

Cole, J. P., & Garvey, T. (2023). *Impeachment and the Constitution (R46013)*. Congressional Research Service. https://www.crsreports.congress.gov

Congressional Research Service. (2020, March 3). *Office of Science and Technology Policy (OSTP): History and overview*. Retrieved March 12, 2024, from https://www.congress.gov/crs-product/R43935

Dator, J. (2006). What is globalization? In J. Dator, D. Pratt, and Y. Seo (Eds.), *Fairness, globalization, and public institutions: East Asia and beyond*. University of Hawai'i Press.

Farrell, C., Hatcher, W., & Diamond, J. (2022). Reflecting on over 100 years of public administration education. *Public Administration, 100*(1), 116–128. https://doi.org/10.1111/padm.12808

Fukuyama, F. (2024). Failing states and failed politics: A call for public administration research. *Public Administration and Development*, 1–3. https://doi.org/10.1002/pad.2049

Haque, M. S., van der Wal, Z., & van den Berg, C. (2021). Comparative studies in public administration: Intellectual challenges and alternative perspectives. *Public Administration Review, 81*(2), 344–348.

Hood, C. (1995). Contemporary public management: a new global paradigm? *Public Policy and Administration, 10*(2), 104–117. https://doi.org/10.1177/095207679501000208

Keohane, R. O., & Nye, J. S. (2000). What's new? What's not? (And so what?). *Foreign Policy, 118*, 104–119.

Lee, B. A. (1982). The New Deal reconsidered. *The Wilson Quarterly* (1976–), 6(2), 62–76. http://www.jstor.org/stable/40256265

Luckey, J. R. (2003, September 10). *OMB circular A-76: Explanation and discussion of the recently revised federal outsourcing policy (RS21489)*. Congressional Research Service.

Leight, M. D. and Abbott, M. (2022). Globalizing public affairs education: The role of comparative public administration in the MPA classroom. *Journal of Public Affairs Education, 28*(4), 373–388.

Nelson, A. K. (1985). President Truman and the evolution of the National Security Council. *The Journal of American History, 72*(2), 360–378. https://doi.org/10.2307/1903380

Office of Science and Technology Policy. (n.d.). *Technology & innovation*. Retrieved March 11, 2024, from https://obamawhitehouse.archives.gov/administration/eop/ostp/divisions/technology

The White House. (n.d.). Promoting innovation and competitiveness: President Bush's technology agenda. Retrieved March 12, 2024, from https://georgebush-whitehouse.archives.gov/infocus/technology

Rearden, S. L. (1984). *History of the secretary of defense: The formative years, 1947-1950*. Historical Office, Office of the Secretary of Defense.

Taylor Society. (1926). Testimony of Frederick W. Taylor at hearings before Special Committee of the House of Representatives, January 1912. *The Taylor Society Journal, 11*(3–4).

Weinberg, M. W. (1983). Public management and private management: A diminishing gap? *Journal of Policy Analysis and Management, 3*(1), 107–115. https://doi.org/10.2307/3324008